Theory and Practice of
Computation

Theory and Practice of
Computation

Proceedings of Workshop on Computation: Theory and Practice WCTP2014

Century Park Hotel, Manila, Philippines
6 – 7 October 2014

Editors

Shin-ya Nishizaki
Tokyo Institute of Technology, Japan

Masayuki Numao
Osaka University, Japan

Jaime D L Caro
University of the Philippines Diliman, Philippines

Merlin Teodosia C Suarez
De La Salle University, Philippines

World Scientific

NEW JERSEY · LONDON · SINGAPORE · BEIJING · SHANGHAI · HONG KONG · TAIPEI · CHENNAI · TOKYO

Published by

World Scientific Publishing Co. Pte. Ltd.
5 Toh Tuck Link, Singapore 596224
USA office: 27 Warren Street, Suite 401-402, Hackensack, NJ 07601
UK office: 57 Shelton Street, Covent Garden, London WC2H 9HE

British Library Cataloguing-in-Publication Data
A catalogue record for this book is available from the British Library.

THEORY AND PRACTICE OF COMPUTATION
Proceedings of Workshop on Computation: Theory and Practice WCTP2014

ISBN 978-981-4725-97-2

Printed in Singapore

PREFACE

Computation should be a good blend of theory and practice. Researchers in the field should create algorithms to address real world problems putting equal weight to analysis and implementation. Experimentation and simulation can be viewed as yielding to refined theories or improved applications. WCTP2014 is the third workshop organized by the Tokyo Institute of Technology, The Institute of Scientific and Industrial Research-Osaka University, University of the Philippines-Diliman and De La Salle University-Manila that is devoted to theoretical and practical approaches to computation. It aims to present the latest developments by theoreticians and practitioners in academe and industry working to address computational problems that can directly impact the way we live in society. Following the success of the Workshop on Computation: Theory and Practice 2011 (WCTP 2011), held in University of the Philippines Diliman, Quezon City, on September 2011, and of WCTP 2012, held in De La Salle University–Manila, on September 2012, WCTP 2013, held both in University of the Philippines Diliman, on September 30 and October 1, 2013 and in University of San Jose-Recoletos, Cebu, on September 28 and 29, 2013, the main and satellite conferences of WCTP 2014 are held both in Century Park Hotel – Manila on October 3, 2014 and in University of the Philippines Cebu, on October 6 and 7, 2014.

This post-proceedings is the collection of the selected papers that were presented at WCTP 2014.

The program of WCTP 2014 was a combination of an invited talk given by Dr. Chikako Morimoto (Tokyo Institute of Technology), and selected research contributions. It included the most recent visions and researches of the invited talk, 6 talks in work-in-progress session, 12 contributions. We collected the original contributions after their presentation at the workshop and began a review procedure that resulted in the selection of the papers in this volume. They appear here in the final form.

WCTP 2014 required a lot of work that was heavily dependent on members of the program committee, and lastly, we owe a great debt of gratitude to the Tokyo Institute of Technology, specifically, its Philippines Office, which is managed by Ronaldo Gallardo, for sponsoring the workhop.

July, 2015

Shin-ya Nishizaki
Masayuki Numao
Jaime Caro
Merlin Teodosia Suarez

PROGRAM CO-CHAIRS

Shin-ya Nishizaki	Tokyo Insitute of Technology, Tokyo, Japan
Masayuki Numao	Osaka University, Osaka, Japan
Jaime Caro	Univeristy of the Philippines – Diliman, the Philippines
Merlin Teodosia Suarez	De La Salle Univeristy – Manila, the Philippines

PROGRAM COMMITTEES

Koichi Moriyama, Ken-ichi Fukui,
— Osaka University, Japan
Satoshi Kurihara, — The University of Electro-Communications, Japan
Ryutaro Ichise — National Institute of Technology, Japan
Mitsuharu Yamamoto — Chiba University, Japan
Hiroyuki Tominaga — Kagawa University, Japan
Naoki Yonezaki, Takuo Watanabe, Shigeki Hagihara
— Tokyo Institute of Technology, Japan
Raymund Sison, Jocelynn Cu, Gregory Cu, Rhia Trogo, Judith Azcarraga, Ethel Ong, Charibeth Cheng, Nelson Marcos, Rafael Cabredo, Joel Ilao
— De La Salle University, the Philippines
Rommel Feria, Henry Adorna, Prospero C. Naval Jr.
— University of the Philippines, the Philippines
John Paul Vergara, Mercedes Rodrigo
— Ateneo De Manila University, the Philippines
Allan A. Sioson — Ateneo de Naga University, the Philippines
Randy S. Gamboa — Univeristy of Southeastern Philippines, the Philippines

GENERAL CO-CHAIRS

Hirofumi Hinode	Tokyo Tech Philippines Office, Tokyo Institute of Technology, Japan
Masayuki Numao	International Collaboration Center, The Institute of Scientific and Industrial Research, Osaka University, Japan

ORGANIZING COMMITTEES

Rafael Cabredo, Joel Ilao, Mary Ruth Delano, Paolo Josef, Christian Magdaong
  – De La Salle University, the Philippines

CONTENTS

SANDAL: A MODELING LANGUAGE SUPPORTING EXHAUSTIVE FAULT-INJECTION

MASAYA SUZUKI[1] and TAKUO WATANABE[2]

Department of Computer Science, Tokyo Institute of Technology,
2-12-1 Ookayama, Meguroku, Tokyo, Japan
E-mail: [1] *draftcode@psg.cs.titech.ac.jp,* [2] *takuo@acm.org*

Sandal is a modeling language designed for specifying and model-checking fault-prone message-passing systems. The language supports the modular description of typical faults including unexpected termination of processes, random loss of messages and timeout. Thus on defining a model in Sandal, one does not need to write such faulty actions explicitly intermingled with the primary behaviors of the model. The compiler of the language automatically weaves them and produces a set of NuSMV modules. This paper describes how the weaving mechanism works and demonstrates the usefulness of the language using an example.

Keywords: modeling language, model checking, fault injection

1. Introduction

Context-awareness gains importance for developing sustainable software systems. In this paper, we take fault-handling as an instance of context-dependent behavior in faulty circumstances and propose a method for describing formal models of fault-prone message-passing systems. Our proposal is a sort of linguistic approach. We designed and developed a modeling language named Sandal that provides abstractions mechanisms for typical faults including unexpected termination of processes and random loss of messages.

To describe a formal model of a system with such faults, one might have to write faulty actions explicitly intermingled with the primary behaviors of the model. We illustrate the situation with an example. Fig. 1 (a) shows a fragment of a simple model written in Promela. Suppose that ch is a channel whose length is more than zero. The model performs actions A or B depending on the value received from the channel. By introducing some fault actions to the model, we gain a faulty version presented in Fig. 1 (b). In this model, a timeout action in receiving a value from ch and

---

(a) A Model Fragment without Faults	(b) A Faulty Version of (a)

```
1  ch ? ans;                          1  bool recv_timeout = false;
2  if                                 2  if
3     :: ans == OK ->                 3     :: ch ? ans
4        A                            4     :: recv_timeout = true
5     :: else ->                      5  fi;
6        B                            6  if
7  fi                                 7     :: ans == OK ->
                                      8        may_shutdown();  A
                                      9     :: else ->
                                     10        may_shutdown();  B
                                     11     :: recv_timeout ->
                                     12        C
                                     13 fi
```

Fig. 1.   Implementing Faulty-Actions in Promela

unexpected process termination actions before A and B are introduced. Both kinds of fault actions are realized using non-deterministic choice. We implement a timeout action (lines 1–5 of Fig. 1 (b)) by adding a choice that skips the reception. The occurrence of the timeout is indicated by the boolean variable recv_timeout using which we can add an extra action C performed on the timeout (lines 11–12). We specify the places where unexpected terminations may happen by inserting may_shutdown() defined as follows into appropriate places of the model.

```
inline may_shutdown() { if :: true :: true -> false fi }
```

The problem we address in this example is that we should inject every observable fault action into its proper place. The task can be tedious and error-prone if performed manually. Moreover, this may increase the size of the resulting model and decrease the maintainability.

We can regard such task — injecting fault actions in their proper places of the model — as an instance of Software Fault Injection (SFI), a method used to improve the coverage of a test. The combination of SFI and model checking is a promising formal approach for verifying software systems in unreliable environments. Towards this direction, tools such as MODIFI[1] and FSAP/NuSMV-SA[2] have been developed. As these tools are designed to treat hardware faults, they are not suitable for our purpose. Furthermore, we cannot solve the modularity problem mentioned above using these existing tools.

We designed a modeling language Sandal that supports the modular description of typical faults including unexpected termination of processes, random loss of messages and timeout[3]. The compiler of the language takes a model and generates a model of its backend model checker (NuSMV[4]). During the compilation process, fault actions specified in the model will be woven into the output. In other words, the compiler performs a sort of software fault-injection (SFI). In this paper, we describe the semantics of the fault-injection as a set of translation rules.

The rest of this paper is organized as follows. The next section gives an overview of our modeling language Sandal. In Section 3, we present the semantics of the fault-injection used in the language as a set of translation rules. Section 4 presents a case study and Section 5 concludes the paper.

2. The Modeling Language Sandal

This section briefly describes the modeling language Sandal. Its syntax loosely follows the tradition of the programming language C. The source code of the compiler (including some sample models) is available at the first author's GitHub repository[a].

Fig. 2 shows a simple Sandal model that describes a system in which two processes exchange messages.

```
proc Starter(recv_ch channel { bool }, send_ch channel { bool }) {
  var v bool
  send(send_ch, true); recv(recv_ch, v)
}
proc Receiver(recv_ch channel { bool }, send_ch channel { bool }) {
  var v bool
  recv(recv_ch, v); send(send_ch, true)
}
init {
  P0: Starter(receiver_to_starter, starter_to_receiver),
  P1: Receiver(starter_to_receiver, receiver_to_starter),
  receiver_to_starter: channel { bool },
  starter_to_receiver: channel { bool },
}
```

Fig. 2.   An Example Model in Sandal

Process Templates A process definition, a construct starting with the keyword **proc**, defines a template of processes. The identifier after **proc** is

[a]https://github.com/draftcode/sandal

the name of the definition. In Fig. 2, two template named `Starter` and `Receiver` are defined. A list of parameters follows after the template name. Both templates in the example have parameters `recv_ch` and `send_ch` of type **channel { bool }** that is a channel of Boolean values. The rest of the process template (a sentence block) will be executed sequentially after the process is instantiated.

Init-Blocks A block beginning with the keyword **init** is called an *init-block*. It describes a configuration of processes and channels in the system to be defined. One can easily change the configuration of the system by modifying the init-block.

An init-block contains several entries (called init-block entries) separated by commas. Each entry must be an instantiation of either a process or a channel. It starts with the name of the instance followed by a colon and the rest part depends on what it represents. If it is an instantiation of a process, a name of a process definition and its arguments follow. If it is an instantiation of a channel, a channel type follows.

Fault markers can be attached to init-block entries. A fault marker attached to a process (or a channel) states that the specified fault may occur in the process (or channel). They are added to the last part of the entries in init-blocks. The current version of Sandal provides two fault markers **@shutdown** and **@drop**.

Messaging Statements Because the statement and expression syntax of Sandal closely matches that of traditional programming languages, we only mention messaging statements in this subsection for brevity. Statements **recv** and **peek** are used for receiving values from a channel. The difference is that **recv** statements pop the values out from a channel while **peek** statements just copy them. These operations have non-blocking and timeout variants.

The arguments to these messaging statements are treated specially. The first argument should be a channel. This is a channel that is used to communicate. The rest of the arguments should be variable names. After the statement is executed, the received values are stored to these variables.

There are two types of channels in Sandal: rendezvous channels and buffered channels. With rendezvous channels, two processes can communicate in a synchronous way; both a sender and a receiver should be ready on the same channel to communicate. With buffered channels, two processes can communicate in an asynchronous way. The values sent are saved in the

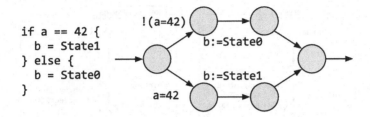

```
if a == 42 {
    b = State1
} else {
    b = State0
}
```

Fig. 3.   Sample Statements and Their Semantics

buffer of a channel. If a receiver want to receive a value, it tries to pop out from the buffer.

3. Fault-Injection Semantics

We give the semantics of Sandal as a set of translation rules to generate NuSMV modules. Every fault specified in the model is translated to a combination of sentences including non-deterministic choices that generates all possible fault scenarios on the fly. In this sense, the translation method is an instance of *exhaustive fault-injection*[5].

3.1. *Processes*

In Sandal, a process is represented as a state machine. Each transition in the state machine may have a condition (called *guard*) and a collection of side-effects (called actions). For example, a guard may be *a value is ready to be received in the channel named c* and an action may be *receive a value in the channel and store it in the variable named v*.

A process is a graph of statements that are executed in order. For example, Fig. 3 shows a composite (**if**) statement and its semantics. There are two branches based on the **if** statement. They are merged into one branch after executing assignment statements. Every statement has semantics like this. The whole process can be expressed in an automaton that is a concatenation of the automata of its statements.

3.2. *Message Sending and Reception*

A pair of **send** and **recv** statements cooperate to exchange messages. Fig. 4 shows the semantics of them. To show the process of this exchange, consider two processes trying to send and receive a value via a rendezvous channel. Sending a value via a rendezvous channel has been done by using three

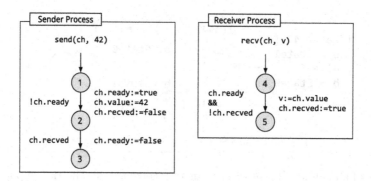

Fig. 4. Two Processes Exchanging a Value

internal variables in a channel: a ready flag, a received flag and a value buffer. The initial states of flags are false. The procedure follows.

(1) In the initial setting, two processes are at state1 and state4, which are shown in the figure. The initial value of the ready flag is false, so the sender process can proceed to state2 while the receiver process cannot proceed to state5.
(2) After the sender process steps to state2, the ready flag is true; and the value, which is about to be sent, is set to the buffer. At this point, the sender process is blocked because the received flag is false and the receiver process can make a step to state5. The receiver process receives a value from the buffer and set the received flag.
(3) The sender process can proceed to state3, and the whole exchange process has been completed.

With this process, only one sender and receiver can communicate in a channel at once, and, even if one process tries to communicate, it blocks until the other process comes to communicate with it.

3.3. *Timeout in Message Reception*

In addition to normal **recv** statement, Sandal provides its variant **timeout_recv**. It is provided as an expression (not a statement) because it returns a Boolean value that will be used to express additional timeout actions.

By invoking a **timeout_recv** expression, a process receives a value from a specified channel. In addition, it may perform a timeout action modeled as the right branch shown in Fig. 5. If a value is successfully received (in

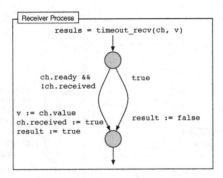

Fig. 5.   `timeout_recv`

Fig. 5), the expression evaluates to true. Otherwise, it evaluates to false.

The expression may perform timeout action even if the corresponding sender process is ready to send a value. This is an intended behavior. Since network delay is unbound, the communication always has a chance to unable to complete a transmission in a specific time window. The behavior of **timeout_recv** expressions reflects these cases.

3.4. *Unexpected Process Termination*

Unexpected termination of processes is a fault that a process is unintentionally shutdown. Using this fault, we can express machine crashes or process crashes. This type of faults will be injected to processes that have **@shutdown** fault markers.

To implement this fault, a shutdown state is introduced and transitions to the state are added in the target process (Fig. 6). These newly added transitions have no guard conditions nor actions. The transitions are injected before and after the execution of statements. This means that each statement is an atomic action, and the termination fault does not interfere with their execution.

This type of fault are also implemented in non-deterministic way; the chance to execute a statement normally and the chance to go to the shutdown state are even. Model checker tries both choices and tries all combination of these choices. By harnessing non-determinism, model checker can simulate arbitrary shutdown scenarios.

8

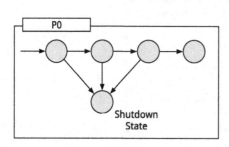

Fig. 6. Injecting Unexpected Terminations of Processes

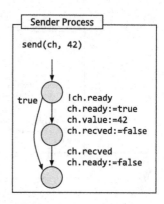

Fig. 7. Injecting a Random Loss of Messages

3.5. *Random Loss of Messages*

Random loss of messages is a fault that some messages are dropped. Thus no receiver will be able to receive them. This type of faults will be injected to channels that have **@drop** fault markers, and all **send** statements over those channels start to drop a message occasionally.

The implementation of this fault is done by modifying the semantics of **send** statements of those faulty channels. The modified **send** statements may skip their normal behavior occasionally (Fig. 7).

4. Case study

As a case study of this work, this section show the modeling and verification of two-phase commit protocol that is an algorithm to solve a consensus problem. It provides a way to determine a value which is acknowledged by all of the machine participated. It is used in major database systems such as MySQL to realize a transaction over multiple nodes.

The algorithm is performed by a single process called an arbiter and two or more processes called workers (Fig. 8). The arbiter initiates the protocol and proposes a value. The workers receive requests from the arbiter and send replies to it. In the first phase of the protocol, the arbiter sends a proposal to the workers. Each worker checks the proposed value and replies whether it is acceptable or not. In the second phase, the arbiter aggregates the replies from the workers and see if all of the workers can accept the proposed value. If the value is acceptable, the arbiter sends a commit message to the workers. The workers received a commit message should accept the proposed value. If one worker replies the value is not acceptable in the first phase, the proposal fails, and the arbiter sends abort messages to the other workers.

In this case study, several models are written in Sandal and Promela. One is the model of two-phase commit protocol without any fault, and the rest is ones with faults. The injected faults are random loss of messages, unexpected termination of processes, and timeout in receiving messages. In each model, the safety property of two-phase commit is verified. A Sandal model with these faults is shown in Fig. 9. Random loss of messages and unexpected termination of processes are injected by adding fault markers and timeout in receiving messages is injected by replacing recv statements of the arbiter with timeout recv statements.

The verification results show both the Sandal models and the Promela models that produce the valid results; the safety property holds for the model without faults and the model with timeout faults. The reason that the property holds with timeout faults is because the models fallback to the abort behavior if the arbiter cannot receive workers' replies. The safety property does not hold for the model with random loss of messages and the model with unexpected termination of processes.

The sizes of the models are measured by lines. Table 1 shows lines of the eight models. Since Sandal has a built-in fault support, the sizes of the models does not grow even if some faults are injected, and the models do not lose their maintainability. The injected faults are well controlled by the

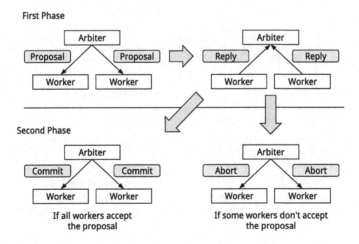

Fig. 8.   Two-Phase Commit Protocol

language so that unwanted side-effects do not occur. The Promela models increase their sizes as some faults are injected. To overcome this issue, an automatic fault-injection tool is needed, but avoiding unwanted side-effects is still hard to accomplish.

Aside from the validity of the verification, the verification speed is also a matter of concern. The benchmark is taken using Linux 3.12.9 running on top of a PC with Intel Core i7-3770K 3.50GHz and 16GB memory. For model checking, we use NuSMV 2.5.4 (as the backend of Sandal) and Spin 6.2.5. The execution times needed to verify the models are shown in Table 2. It shows the verification speed of Sandal is still acceptable even if some faults are injected. It is interesting that the speed is increased or decreased when injecting faults in Sandal while there are no differences among the speeds of the Spin models. The reason for this is considered to be the difference of the model checking algorithms. NuSMV, the backend of Sandal, does symbolic model checking while Spin does explicit model checking.

The resources consumed in the verifications are shown in Table 3 and Table 4. They show the number of the BDD nodes allocated by NuSMV and the number of the states stored by Spin respectively.

No significant relationships between the BDD node sizes and the verification speeds can be observed. The number of states in some Promela models are very small. This is because Spin stops verification when it find the first counter-example.

	Sandal	Promela		Sandal	Spin
No fault	51	66	No fault	0.96	1.01
w/Timeout	51	74	w/Timeout	2.88	1.02
w/Message loss	51	70	w/Message loss	2.11	1.06
w/Termination	51	98	w/Termination	0.51	1.17

No fault	925483	No fault	110
w/Timeout	261547	w/Timeout	305
w/Message loss	369272	w/Message loss	11
w/Termination	588751	w/Termination	7

```
data Response { Ready, NotReady, Commit, Abort }
proc Arbiter(chRecvs []channel { Response },
             chSends []channel { Response }) {
  var determined bool = false
  for ch in chSends {
    send(ch, Ready)
  }
  var all_ready bool = true
  for ch in chRecvs {
    var resp Response
    var recved bool = timeout_recv(ch, resp)
    if !recved || (recved && resp != Ready) {
      all_ready = false
    }
  }
  determined = true
  if all_ready {
    for ch in chSends { send(ch, Commit) }
  } else {
    for ch in chSends { send(ch, Abort) }
  }
}
proc Worker(chRecv channel { Response }, chSend channel { Response }) {
  var resp Response
  recv(chRecv, resp)
  choice { send(chSend, NotReady) }, { send(chSend, Ready) }
  recv(chRecv, resp)
}
init {
  chWorker1Send : channel { Response } @drop,
  chWorker1Recv : channel { Response } @drop,
  chWorker2Send : channel { Response } @drop,
  chWorker2Recv : channel { Response } @drop,
  arbiter : Arbiter([chWorker1Send, chWorker2Send],
                    [chWorker1Recv, chWorker2Recv]) @shutdown,
  worker1 : Worker(chWorker1Recv, chWorker1Send) @shutdown,
  worker2 : Worker(chWorker2Recv, chWorker2Send) @shutdown,
}
ltl {
  F (G (arbiter.determined &&
    ((!arbiter.all_ready) ->
        (!(worker1.resp == Commit) && !(worker2.resp == Commit)))))
}
```

Fig. 9. A Two-Phase Commit Model in Sandal

12

5. Concluding Remark

We propose a linguistic approach to reducing the cost of modeling fault-prone distributed systems. The key technology is a variation of software fault injection (SFI) applied to process models used for model checking. We designed and implemented a modeling language Sandal that supports the specification of typical faults in message-passing systems. Using the Sandal compiler, all possible faults specified in a model is automatically injected into the result that can be model checked by NuSMV. The advantage of the method is demonstrated by specifying and verifying models of the two-phase commit protocol.

ReferencesReferences

1. R. Svenningsson, J. Vinter, H. Eriksson and M. Törngren, MODIFI: A MODel-Implemented Fault Injection tool, in *Computer Safety, Reliability, and Security*, , Lecture Notes in Computer Science Vol. 6351 (Springer-Verlag, 2010).
2. M. Bozzano and A. Villafiorita, Improving system reliability via model checking: The FSAP/NuSMV-SA safety analysis platform, in *Computer Safety, Reliability, and Security (SAFECOMP 2003)*, , Lecture Notes in Computer Science Vol. 2788 (Springer-Verlag, 2003).
3. M. Suzuki and T. Watanabe, A language support for exhaustive fault-injection in message-passing system models, in *1st Workshop on Logics and MODel-checking for self-* systems (MOD* 2014)*, , Electronic Proceedings in Theoretical Computer Science Vol. 168, 2014.
4. A. Cimatti, E. Clarke, E. Giunchiglia, F. Giunchiglia, M. Pistore, M. Roveri, R. Sebastiani and A. Tacchella, NuSMV 2: An opensource tool for symbolic model checking, in *Computer Aided Verification*, , Lecture Notes in Computer Science Vol. 2404 (Springer-Verlag, 2002).
5. W. Steiner, J. Rushby, M. Sorea and H. Pfeifer, Model checking a fault-tolerant startup algorithm: From design exploration to exhaustive fault simulation, in *International Conference on Dependable Systems and Networks (DSN '04)*, 2004.

AN EFFICIENT IMPLEMENTATION
OF SATISFIABILITY CHECKING FOR LTL
WITH MEAN-PAYOFF CONSTRAINTS

Takashi Tomita, Takahito Kimura, Shigeki Hagihara and Naoki Yonezaki

Department of Information Science and Engineering, Tokyo Institute of Technology,
2-12-1 Ookayama, Meguro-ku, Tokyo 152-8550, Japan
Phone and Fax: +81-3-5734-2772
E-mail: {tomita, hagihara, yonezaki}@fmx.cs.titech.ac.jp,
kimura@lambda.cs.titech.ac.jp

Functional aspects of the behavioral properties of systems are the main concern in formal verification. However, performance aspects of them are also important. LTL^{mp} is an LTL extension with expressions about mean-payoff. This logic expresses not only qualitative and functional properties of patterns of event occurrences but also quantitative properties of average performance, such as the long-run frequency of event occurrences. In this paper, we introduce an efficient procedure for LTL^{mp} satisfiability checking. The procedure consists of (1) parsing and normalizing a given LTL^{mp} formula, and transforming it into a combination of LTL parts and mean-payoff parts, (2) translating the LTL parts into transition-based generalized Büchi automata (TGBAs), (3) decomposing the automata into accepting strongly connected components (SCCs), (4) interpreting combinations of the mean-payoff parts and the SCCs into formulae of the quantifier-free linear real arithmetic (LRA) theory, and then (5) deciding the satisfiability of the LRA formulae and that of the given LTL^{mp} formula. We implemented the procedure and confirmed the effectiveness of our implementation through some experiments.

Keywords: Specification verification; Temporal logic; LTL extension; Mean payoff; Satisfiability.

1. Introduction

In formal verification, functional aspects of the behavioral properties of systems have been the main concern because they are the basis of the reliability and security of systems. *Linear Temporal Logic*[1] (LTL) can represent qualitative properties concerning the order (or pattern) of event occurrences, and most of natural and functional requirements for systems are such properties. LTL is widely used as a specification language in many *model-checking*[2] systems.

In practice, performance analysis is also important in developing systems with higher quality. For the formal verification of both functional and performance properties, we developed LTL^{mp}, which is a *mean-payoff* extension of LTL, and algorithms to solve decision and optimization problems for it.[3] The mean-payoff constraint expressed in LTL^{mp} is a threshold condition for the limit inferior of mean-payoffs under a given payoff setting, and can capture quantitative properties of, *e.g.*, the long-run frequency of event occurrences and long-run average of costs. However, there is no implementation for the algorithms.

In this paper, we improve a procedure for checking the *satisfiability* (or *consistency*) of an LTL^{mp} formula, which was described originally in Ref. 3. The outline of the improved procedure is as follows: (1) parsing and normalizing a given LTL^{mp} formula, and transforming it into a disjunction of conjunctive pairs of LTL parts and mean-payoff parts, (2) translating the LTL parts into *transition-based generalized Büchi automata*[4] (TGBAs), (3) decomposing the automata into *strongly connected components* (SCCs) and extracting accepting ones, (4) interpreting combinations of the mean-payoff parts and the components of the automata translated from their corresponding LTL parts into formulae of the (quantifier-free) *linear real arithmetic* (LRA) theory, and then (5) deciding the satisfiability of the LRA formulae and that of the given LTL^{mp} formula. Our improved procedure uses TGBAs, while *Büchi automata* (BAs) were used in the original procedure in Ref. 3. A TGBA translated from an LTL formula is mostly smaller than a BA translated from the same LTL formula,[4] and hence using TGBAs is often more efficient than using BAs in verification based on automata-theoretic approach.[5] Our procedure is based on automata-theoretic approach, and thus the speedup by using TGBA is expected.

We implemented the procedure and confirmed the effectiveness of our implementation through some experiments. In our implementation, we used existing efficient tools, an LTL-to-automata translator and a *satisfiability modulo theory* (SMT) solver, for Steps 2 and 5, respectively. Step 1 and 4 are simple transformations. The decomposition in Step 3 can be performed efficiently with techniques used widely in graph theory.

Related work. We also developed model-checking and optimization algorithms for LTL^{mp}.[3] LTL^{mp} model-checking can be used for mean-payoff performance analysis of a given model. LTL^{mp} optimization seeks to optimize an objective function specified by a mean-payoff term in LTL^{mp} under a given LTL^{mp} formula. This optimization can be used for theoretical limitation analysis of the mean-payoff performance of systems under a given specification.

Independently of the study of LTL^{mp}, Bohy et $al.$ introduced LTL$_{\mathrm{MP}}$, which is another mean-payoff extension of LTL and is a strict subset of LTL^{mp}, and a $realizability$[6,7] checker Acacia+ (ver. 2.3^{a}) to support it.[8] Realizability is a property that there exists an $open$ (or $reactive$) system satisfying a given specification, whereas satisfiability can be viewed as a property that there exists a $closed$ system satisfying a given specification; therefore, realizability is a stronger property than satisfiability.

The rest of this paper. In Sec. 2, we introduce LTL^{mp}, BAs and TGBAs. In Sec. 3, we briefly explain the improved procedure of LTL^{mp} satisfiability checking. In Sec. 4, we describe an implementation of the procedure, and show the effectiveness of our implementation by experiments. In Sec. 5, we provide our conclusions.

2. Preliminaries

2.1. *LTL^{mp}*

Linear Temporal Logic (LTL) is a modal logic with *logical connectives* ($\neg$ and $\vee$) in propositional logic and *temporal operators* $\mathbf{X}$ and $\mathbf{U}$.[1] Intuitively, $\mathbf{X}\psi_1$ means "ψ_1 holds in the $neXt$ step," and $\psi_1\mathbf{U}\psi_2$ means "ψ_2 eventually holds and ψ_1 holds $Until$ then," where ψ_1 and ψ_2 are LTL formulae. $\top \equiv \psi_1 \vee \neg\psi_1$, $\bot \equiv \neg\top$, $\psi_1 \wedge \psi_2 \equiv \neg(\neg\psi_1 \vee \neg\psi_2)$, $\psi_1 \rightarrow \psi_2 \equiv \neg\psi_1 \vee \psi_2$, $\psi_1 \leftrightarrow \psi_2 \equiv (\psi_1 \rightarrow \psi_2) \wedge (\psi_2 \rightarrow \psi_1)$, $\mathbf{F}\psi_1 \equiv \top\mathbf{U}\psi_1$ ("ψ_1 holds in the $Future$"), $\mathbf{G}\psi_1 \equiv \neg\mathbf{F}\neg\psi_1$ ("ψ_1 holds $Globally$") and $\psi_1\mathbf{R}\psi_2 \equiv \neg(\neg\psi_1\mathbf{U}\neg\psi_2)$ ("ψ_1 $Releases$ ψ_2") are commonly used as abbreviations. The symbols $\bigcirc$, $\Diamond$ and $\square$ are often used instead of $\mathbf{X}$, $\mathbf{F}$ and $\mathbf{G}$, respectively.

LTL^{mp} is a mean-payoff extension of LTL.[3] A *mean-payoff formula* θ in LTL^{mp} is a threshold condition for the limit inferior $\mathbf{MP}(t)$ of the average of payoffs under a given payoff setting. A payoff setting is given as a term t representing a value ($i.e.$, payoff) at each step, based on temporal properties that hold at the moment. Formally, θ and t have the following forms, respectively:

$$\theta ::= \mathbf{MP}(t) \sim c, \tag{1}$$

$$t ::= \mathbf{1}_\psi \mid t_1 + t_2 \mid t_1 \cdot t_2 \mid -t_1 \mid c \cdot t_1, \tag{2}$$

where $\sim \in \{<, >, \leq, \geq\}$ is a standard comparison operator, $c \in \mathbb{R}$ is a real constant, ψ is an LTL formula, $\mathbf{1}_\psi$ is a *characteristic variable*. In Ref. 3, a

---

^{a}Available at http://lit2.ulb.ac.be/acaciaplus/

term is defined with also other types of variables to refer to weights on a model, for model checking. We omit them in this paper because they are almost meaningless in satisfiability checking.

For each step, a characteristic variable $\mathbf{1}_\psi$ assigns 1 if ψ holds, otherwise 0. Because a negative payoff is available in LTL^{mp}, we can express a threshold condition for the limit superior of mean-payoffs, and use an abbreviation $\overline{\mathbf{MP}}(t) \sim c \equiv \mathbf{MP}(-t)\widetilde{\sim} - c$, where $\widetilde{\sim}$ is < (>, ≤, ≥) when $\sim$ is > (<, ≥, ≤).

An LTL^{mp} formula is given by a combination of logical connectives and temporal operators, on a set AP of atomic propositions and a set of mean-payoff formulae derived from LTL on AP. The *satisfaction relation* $\models$ between an ω-word $\sigma = a_0a_1\ldots \in (2^{AP})^\omega$ and an LTL^{mp} formula φ is inductively defined in the usual LTL manner for logical connectives and temporal operators. For mean-payoff formulae, it is defined as follows:

$$\sigma \models \mathbf{MP}(t) \sim c \Leftrightarrow \liminf_{i\to\infty} \frac{1}{i+1} \cdot \sum_{j=0}^{i} [\![t]\!]_\sigma(j) \sim c, \tag{3}$$

where $[\![t]\!]_\sigma : \mathbb{N} \to \mathbb{R}$ is a function that assigns a payoff at each step as follows:

$$[\![\mathbf{1}_\psi]\!]_\sigma(j) = \begin{cases} 1 & \text{if } a_ja_{j+1}\ldots \models \psi, \\ 0 & \text{otherwise,} \end{cases} \tag{4}$$

$$[\![t_1 + t_2]\!]_\sigma(j) = [\![t_1]\!]_\sigma(j) + [\![t_2]\!]_\sigma(j), \tag{5}$$

$$[\![t_1 \cdot t_2]\!]_\sigma(j) = [\![t_1]\!]_\sigma(j) \cdot [\![t_2]\!]_\sigma(j), \tag{6}$$

$$[\![-t_1]\!]_\sigma(j) = -[\![t_1]\!]_\sigma(j), \tag{7}$$

$$[\![c \cdot t_1]\!]_\sigma(j) = c \cdot [\![t_1]\!]_\sigma(j), \tag{8}$$

where ψ is an LTL formula. As can be seen in Eq. (3), the mean-payoff formula can be considered to represent the properties of long-run suffixes of words.

An LTL^{mp} formula φ is *satisfiable* if there exists a word $\sigma \in (2^{AP})^\omega$ such that $\sigma \models \varphi$.

2.2. Büchi Automata

An ω-*automaton* is a transition machine that decides either to accept or reject an ω-word. Formally, an ω-automaton is defined as a quintuple $\mathcal{A} = \langle Q, \Sigma, \delta, q_0, \mathcal{F} \rangle$, where Q is a finite *set of states*, Σ is a finite *alphabet*, $\delta \subseteq Q \times \Sigma \times Q$ is a *transition relation* between states with a label in Σ, $q_0 \in Q$ is the *initial state*, and $\mathcal{F}$ specifies an acceptance condition. For an input word $\sigma = a_0 a_1 \ldots \in \Sigma^\omega$, a *run* $\gamma = \langle q_0, a_0, q_1 \rangle \langle q_1, a_1, q_2 \rangle \ldots \in \delta^\omega$ is an infinite sequence of transitions, if it exists. That is, σ is a sequence of labels on γ. Generally, there exist multiple runs derived from a word because the transition relation δ may be nondeterministic. Automaton $\mathcal{A}$ decides to accept or to reject a run, according to an acceptance condition based on $\mathcal{F}$. $\mathcal{A}$ *accepts* a word deriving at least one accepting run. A set of all words accepted by $\mathcal{A}$ is a language *recognized* by $\mathcal{A}$. Automata are *equivalent* if they recognize the same language.

A *Büchi automaton* (BA) is an ω-automaton that recognizes an ω-regular language, the class of which is a superset of a class of languages specified by LTL. In a BA, $\mathcal{F}$ is given by a *set* $Q' \subseteq Q$ *of acceptance states*, and a run γ is *accepted* if at least one state in $\mathcal{F}$ is infinitely often visited on γ, *i.e.*, at least one acceptance state is visited on any suffix of γ (*Büchi condition*).

Transition-based generalized Büchi automata. A *transition-based generalized Büchi automaton*[4] (TGBA) is a variant of BA. In a TGBA, $\mathcal{F}$ is given by a *family of sets* $\delta_1, \ldots, \delta_n \subseteq \delta$ *of acceptance transitions*, and a run γ is *accepted* if at least one transition in δ_i appears infinitely often on γ for each $\delta_i \in \mathcal{F}$.

For a BA with state space Q, there exists an equivalent TGBA with state space Q' such that $|Q'| \leq |Q|$. It is explained by the fact that a BA $\langle Q, \Sigma, \delta, q_0, Q' \rangle$ is equivalent to a TGBA $\langle Q, \Sigma, \delta, q_0, \{\delta'\} \rangle$ where δ' is a set $\{\langle q_1, a, q_2 \rangle \in \delta \mid q_1 \in Q'\}$ of outgoing transitions from Q'.

A smaller automaton can be analyzed more efficiently in many cases, and therefore it is expected that using TGBA is more effective than using BA in analysis via automata.

Strongly connected components. A subgraph $\langle Q', \delta' \rangle \subseteq \langle Q, \delta \rangle$ is a *strongly-connected component* (SCC) if it is a maximal subgraph consisting of states that are reachable from each other. An SCC $\langle Q', \delta' \rangle$ is *trivial* if $\delta' = \emptyset$. A non-trivial SCC $\langle Q', \delta' \rangle$ is *accepting* if $Q' \cap \mathcal{F} \neq \emptyset$ when $\mathcal{A}$ is a BA, and if $\delta' \cap \delta_i \neq \emptyset$ for all $\delta_i \in \mathcal{F}$ when $\mathcal{A}$ is a TGBA.

Because any run reaches eventually to and stays forever in a certain SCC, accepting SCCs capture long-run suffixes of accepting runs (and words).

LTL-to-automata translation. An LTL formula ψ on a set AP of atomic propositions represents a language as a set $\{\sigma \in (2^{AP})^\omega \mid \sigma \models \psi\}$ of words satisfying ψ, and thus ψ is *equivalent* to an automaton whose alphabet is 2^{AP} and which recognizes the language.

For an LTL formula ψ, we can construct an equivalent BA (or TGBA) whose state space is exponentially bounded for the size of ψ, *i.e.*, ψ can be translated into the BA (or TGBA).[4,9,10] For example, an LTL formula **GF**$a \wedge$ **GF**b is equivalent to a BA and a TGBA in Fig. 1 (left and right, respectively), where a node and a directed edge represent a state and a transition, respectively, a label of an edge is represented by a Boolean expression on AP, a doubled node represents an accepting state of the BA, and an annotated number of a transition of the TGBA represents an index for sets of accepting transitions.

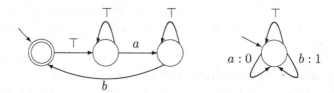

Fig. 1.   A BA (left) and a TGBA (right) equivalent to an LTL formula **GF**$a \wedge$ **GF**b.

3. Procedure

In this section, we briefly explain an improved procedure for checking whether a given LTL^{mp} formula φ is satisfiable. The LTL^{mp} satisfiability problem is in EXPTIME for the size of φ and the number of mean-payoff formulae in φ.[3]

The satisfiability of an LTL^{mp} formula can be reduced to the nonemptiness of a kind of weighted BA corresponding to the LTL^{mp} formula.[3] It is not necessary to construct explicitly such a weighted BA and, hence, we retain information about a BA and weights (*i.e.*, payoffs) separately. BAs are used in the original procedure in Ref. 3, however, we use TGBAs in this paper.

The improved procedure consists of the following steps.

(1) Parsing and normalizing a given LTL^{mp} formula φ, and transforming it into a disjunction of conjunctive pairs of LTL parts and mean-payoff parts.

(2) Translating the LTL parts into TGBAs.

(3) Decomposing the automata into SCCs and extracting accepting ones.

(4) Interpreting combinations of the mean-payoff parts and the accepting SCCs of the automata translated from their corresponding LTL parts into formulae of (quantifier-free) *linear real arithmetic* (LRA) theory.

(5) Deciding the satisfiability of the LRA formulae and that of φ.

The differences between the original procedure in Ref. 3 and the improved procedure are just a type of automata in Step 2 and how to extract accepting SCCs in Step 3. Thus, the correctness of the improved procedure is trivial.

The time complexity of Steps 3-5 depends on the sizes of the automata translated in Step 2,[3] and they are exponential in the sizes of (LTL parts of) φ. Thus, the speedup of the procedure is expected by using TGBA because TGBAs have smaller state spaces than those of BAs.

In the rest of this section, we briefly explain each step of the improved procedure.

Step 1. After parsing the input LTL^{mp} formula, first, fresh atomic propositions are introduced. For n characteristic variables $\mathbf{1}_{\psi_1}, \ldots, \mathbf{1}_{\psi_n}$ of LTL subformulae $\psi_1, \ldots, \psi_n$ with temporal operators in φ, n fresh atomic propositions $p_{\psi_1}, \ldots, p_{\psi_n}$ are introduced. Let AP_φ be the extended set of atomic propositions including fresh ones, and $\varphi' = \varphi[p_{\psi_1}, \ldots, p_{\psi_n}/\psi_1, \ldots, \psi_n]$ be an LTL^{mp} formula with substitution of $p_{\psi_1}, \ldots, p_{\psi_n}$ for $\psi_1, \ldots, \psi_n$ in φ, respectively.

Second, an additional LTL formula $\psi_{\mathrm{bind}} = \bigwedge_{1 \leq i \leq n} \mathbf{G}(p_{\psi_i} \leftrightarrow \psi_i)$ to bind every pair of p_{ψ_i} and ψ_i is introduced. A word $\sigma \in (2^{AP})^\omega$ corresponds one-to-one to extended one $\sigma' \in (2^{AP_\varphi})^\omega$ satisfying ψ_{bind}, and σ satisfies φ if and only if σ' satisfies $\varphi' \wedge \psi_{\mathrm{bind}}$. Note that a function $[\![\mathbf{1}_{\psi_i}]\!]_\sigma$ of payoffs on σ for $\mathbf{1}_{\psi_i}$ corresponds to a sequence of truth values for p_{ψ_i} on σ', because p_{ψ_i} predicts whether ψ_i holds at each step if σ' satisfies ψ_{bind}.

Third, $\varphi' \wedge \psi_{\mathrm{bind}}$ is transformed into a disjunction of 2^n conjunctive pairs of LTL parts and mean-payoff parts as follows:

$$\bigvee_{b_1, \ldots, b_m \in \mathbb{B}} \Big(\overbrace{\varphi'[b_1, \ldots, b_m/\theta_1, \ldots, \theta_m] \wedge \psi_{\mathrm{bind}}}^{\text{LTL part}} \wedge \overbrace{\bigwedge_{1 \leq j \leq m} \theta_j^{b_j}}^{\text{Mean-payoff part}} \Big), \qquad (9)$$

where $\mathbb{B} = \{\top, \bot\}$ is a Boolean domain, $\theta_1, \ldots, \theta_m$ are m mean-payoff formulae in φ', and, for $\theta = \mathbf{MP}(t) \sim c$, θ^b is $\mathbf{MP}(t) \sim c$ if $b = \top$, otherwise $\mathbf{MP}(t) \not\sim c$, where $\not\sim$ is $<$ ($>$, $\leq$, $\geq$) when $\sim$ is $\geq$ ($\leq$, $>$, $<$). This transformation is valid because $\mathbf{F}\theta \Leftrightarrow \mathbf{G}\theta$ is valid from Eq. (3).[3]

Equation (9) is a normalized (and extended) LTL^{mp} formula of φ. φ is satisfiable if and only if Eq. (9) is satisfiable.

Step 2. Each LTL part in the normalized LTL^{mp} formula is translated into an automaton, by the technique of LTL-to-automata translation.[4,9,10]

Let $\mathcal{A}^{\varphi}_{b_1,\ldots,b_m} = \langle Q, 2^{AP_{\varphi}}, \delta, q_0, \mathcal{F} \rangle$ be a TGBA translated from an LTL part $\varphi'[b_1,\ldots,b_m/\theta_1,\ldots,\theta_m] \wedge \psi_{\mathrm{bind}}$.

Step 3. Each automaton is decomposed efficiently into a set of SCCs with general algorithms in graph theory: *e.g.*, Tarjan's algorithm.

For the automaton $\mathcal{A}^{\varphi}_{b_1,\ldots,b_m}$ with SCCs $\langle Q'_1, \delta'_1 \rangle, \ldots, \langle Q'_l, \delta'_l \rangle \subseteq \langle Q, \delta \rangle$, we can readily extract a set of accepting SCCs. The extraction of accepting SCCs on TGBAs is different but similar to that for BAs, and the other steps of the procedure are the same as when using BAs.

Step 4. On automata, the long-run frequency of transition (or its label) occurrences on an accepting run equals that on a long-run suffix of the run. The long-run suffix consists of a combination of cycles in a certain accepting SCC.

Thus, the possibility of existence of a run that (a) satisfies a mean-payoff part $\bigwedge_{1 \leq j \leq m} \theta_j^{b_j}$ and (b) reaches eventually to and stays forever in the k-th accepting SCC $\langle Q'_k, \delta'_k \rangle$ on the automaton $\mathcal{A}^{\varphi}_{b_1,\ldots,b_m}$ translated from their corresponding LTL part, is reduced to the satisfiability of a conjunction of $\mathcal{O}(m)$ LRA formulae. These LRA formulae are independent from each other, and each represents a conjunction of

(i) a condition for the transition (or its label) occurrence ratio that satisfies a certain subpart of the mean-payoff part, and
(ii) a condition for the ratio that represents a combination of cycles in the SCC.

The details of the LRA formulae are omitted in this paper (see Ref. 3 for details). As a supplemental explanation, each of the LRA formulae is a conjunction of $\mathcal{O}(m) + (|Q'_k| + 1)$ constraints for conditions (i) and (ii), on $|\delta'_k|$ non-negative real variables associated with transitions in δ'_k. We can reduce the size (*i.e.*, numbers of the variables and constraints) of the LRA formulae if some variables are linear-dependent and if some constraints are weaker than others.

An example of an LRA formula interpreted in Step 4. Consider an accepting SCC $\langle Q', \delta' \rangle$ in Fig. 2 and a mean-payoff formula $\mathbf{MP}(1_a) \geq$

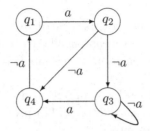

Fig. 2. An example accepting SCC (where accepting transitions or states are omitted).

$1/2$, where $Q' = \{q_1, \ldots, q_4\}$ and $\delta' = \{\langle q_1, \{a\}, q_2\rangle, \langle q_2, \emptyset, q_3\rangle, \langle q_2, \emptyset, q_4\rangle,$
$\langle q_3, \emptyset, q_3\rangle, \langle q_3, \{a\}, q_4\rangle, \langle q_4, \emptyset, q_1\rangle\}$.

We use non-negative variables $x_1, \ldots, x_6$ representing the number of occurrence of transitions $\langle q_1, \{a\}, q_2\rangle$, $\langle q_2, \emptyset, q_3\rangle$, $\langle q_2, \emptyset, q_4\rangle$, $\langle q_3, \emptyset, q_3\rangle$, $\langle q_3, \{a\}, q_4\rangle$ and $\langle q_4, \emptyset, q_1\rangle$, respectively. Using these variables, an LRA formula interpreted from $\langle Q', \delta'\rangle$ and $\mathbf{MP}(1_a) \geq 1/2$ is given as a conjunction of linear constraints as follows:

$$x_1 + x_5 \geq x_2 + x_3 + x_4 + x_6, \tag{10}$$
$$x_1 + x_2 + x_3 + x_4 + x_5 + x_6 > 0, \tag{11}$$
$$x_6 = x_1, \tag{12}$$
$$x_1 = x_2 + x_3, \tag{13}$$
$$x_2 = x_5, \tag{14}$$
$$x_5 = x_6. \tag{15}$$

The mean-payoff condition (i) is represented by Eq. (10) which means that the occurrence number of a-labeled transitions is greater than a half of the total occurrence number of transitions. The cyclicity condition (ii) is represented by Eq. (11)-(15). Equation (11) means that the total occurrence number of transitions is positive. Equation (12)-(15) means that the occurrence number of incoming transitions is equal to that of outgoing transitions for each state.

The LRA formula has a solution, *e.g.*, $\langle x_1, \ldots, x_6\rangle = \langle 1, 1, 0, 0, 1, 1\rangle$. This solution represents a cycle $\langle q_1, \{a\}, q_2\rangle\langle q_2, \emptyset, q_3\rangle\langle q_3, \{a\}, q_4\rangle\langle q_4, \emptyset, q_1\rangle$ which may have no accepting transition (or accepting state). However, this is a witness of the existence of an accepting run satisfying $\mathbf{MP}(1_a) \geq 1/2$ because there exists a cycle on which the ratio of transition occurrences converges to the solution and transitions d_3 and d_4 occur infinitely and negligibly often, *i.e.*, all transitions and states (including accepting ones) occur infinitely often.

Step 5. Consequently, there exists a satisfiable conjunction of LRA formulae interpreted from (a) a mean-payoff part and (b) an accepting SCC of their corresponding automaton, if and only if the input LTL^{mp} formula φ is satisfiable.

The satisfiability of each LRA formula is decided with a solving technique for *satisfiability modulo theory* (SMT) problems in polynomial time for the size of the LRA formula.

4. Implementation and Experiments

4.1. *Implementation*

We have implemented the procedure in Sec. 3, using Python (ver. 2.7.8). In the implementation, we used the following tools and a Python library.

- Antlr (ver. 3.4[b]) to generate a parser for LTL^{mp},
- LTL3BA [10] (ver. 1.0.2[c]) to translate LTL formulae into (TG)BAs,
- NetworkX (ver. 1.7[d]) which is a Python library, for graph manipulation including SCC decomposition, and
- Yices [11] (ver. 2.1.0[e]) as an SMT solver for the LRA theory.

In the implementation, we can select a type (BA or TGBA) of automata translated form LTL formulae, and Steps 4 and 5 are repeated for each pair of (a) a mean-payoff part and (b) an accepting SCC of their corresponding automaton. Additionally, the number of variables in an LRA formula can be reduced if linear dependency among some of the variables is found by a superficial analysis of a coefficient matrix of the LRA formula.

4.2. *Experiments*

We conducted some experiments to show the effectiveness of our implementation. A discussion of the experimental results is provided in Sec. 4.3.

As input LTL^{mp} formulae, we used parameterized ones $\varphi_{\mathrm{elv1}}(n) = \psi_{\mathrm{elv}}(n) \wedge \theta_1$ and $\varphi_{\mathrm{elv2}}(n) = \psi_{\mathrm{elv}}(n) \wedge (\bigwedge_{2 \le i \le 4} \theta_i) \wedge \theta_5(n)$, where an LTL formula $\psi_{\mathrm{elv}}(n)$ is a functional specification and mean-payoff formulae $\theta_1, \ldots, \theta_4$ and $\theta_5(n)$ are performance specifications. Precise definitions of the LTL and mean-payoff formulae are given in App. A. For these input

[b] Available at http://www.antlr3.org
[c] Available at http://sourceforge.net/projects/ltl3ba/
[d] Available at https://networkx.github.io/index.html
[e] Available at http://yices.csl.sri.com/

Table 1. Experimental result for $\varphi_{\text{elv1}}(n)$ with a single mean-payoff formula.

Automata Type	n	Execution Time (sec)				Automaton		LRA Variables
		Step 2	Step 4	Step 5	Total	States	Transitions	
BA	2	0.02	0.51	0.05	0.63	42	283	558
	3	0.36	7.75	2.94	11.33	263	3891	7762
	4	6.20	-	-	-	1654	54091	108130
	5	310.72	-	-	-	10400	696451	-
TGBA	2	0.05	0.13	0.06	0.29	26	185	362
	3	0.24	1.29	0.94	2.81	118	2222	4421
	4	6.69	18.00	109.60	139.10	585	25989	51913
	5	300.90	-	-	-	3025	282724	565286

Table 2. Experimental result for $\varphi_{\text{elv2}}(n)$ with 4 mean-payoff formulae.

Automata Type	n	Execution Time (sec)				Automaton		LRA Variables
		Step 2	Step 4	Step 5	Total	States	Transitions	
BA	2	0.01	3.00	0.64	3.87	23	158	610
	3	0.16	-	-	-	182	2866	12188
	4	5.90	-	-	-	1385	46801	-
TGBA	2	0.03	1.10	0.71	2.07	17	134	629
	3	0.17	16.85	163.98	181.70	88	1829	8536
	4	8.36	-	-	-	495	23181	107301

LTL^{mp} formulae, each of their normalized and extended LTL^{mp} formulae will be a pair of an LTL formula and a conjunction of mean-payoff formulae. The experiments were performed on a MacBook Air (Intel Core i7 2GHz Ivy-Bridge CPU, 8GB RAM, Mac OSX 10.9.4).

The experimental results for $\varphi_{\text{elv1}}(n)$ and $\varphi_{\text{elv2}}(n)$ are shown in Table 1 and 2, respectively. In each of the tables, we list the execution times of Step 2, 4, 5 and the whole procedure, the number of states and transitions of an automaton translated from the LTL part, and the number of variables in LRA formulae. Following the standard manner about the size of automata, multiple non-acceptance transitions between states are considered as a single transition between the states. The hyphen "-" means a lack of data because of timeout (10 min). All completed executions output "satisfiable."

4.3. Discussion

First, we consider the capability of our implementation. Table 1 and 2 indicate that our implementation can handle some LTL^{mp} formulae such that automata translated from LTL parts of them have dozens of thousands of transitions (more precisely, LRA variables).

Second, we consider the effectiveness of using TGBAs. The whole executions using TGBA were completed in shorter time than those using BA.

24

Especially, Steps 4 and 5 using TGBA were much faster than those using BA in most cases. Given this, we confirmed the effectiveness of using TGBAs. The minimization of automata was not strict in the experiments; however, tighter minimization may be effective.

5. Conclusions

We improved a procedure for the satisfiability checking for LTL^{mp} which is an LTL extension to express quantitative properties of performance requirements about mean payoffs. The improved procedure using TGBAs was more efficient than the original one using BAs because TGBAs have smaller state spaces than those of BAs.

Moreover, we implemented the improved procedure. In our implementation, we used existing efficient tools, an LTL-to-automata translator and an SMT solver, for translating LTL formulae into automata and solving the satisfiability of LRA formulae, respectively. We confirmed the effectiveness of using TGBAs and indicated that our implementation can handle some LTL^{mp} formulae such that automata translated from LTL parts of them have dozens of thousands of transitions.

Future work. One future aim is to improve our implementation, *e.g.*, to support the parallelization of the satisfiability checking for LRA formulae defined from a subpart of a normalized LTL^{mp} formula. Because the satisfiability of these LRA formulae is independent of each other, parallelization should be effective and easily introduced.

Another target is to implement procedures for model-checking and optimization for LTL^{mp}, the algorithms for which are given in Ref. 3 and are similar to the satisfiability checking for LTL^{mp}.

References

1. A. Pnueli, The temporal logic of programs, in *Foundations of Computer Science, 1977., 18th Annual Symposium on*, (IEEE, 1977) pp. 46–57.
2. E. M. Clarke, E. A. Emerson and A. P. Sistla, Automatic verification of finite-state concurrent systems using temporal logic specifications, *ACM Transaction on Programming Languages and Systems* **8(2)**, 244 (1986).
3. T. Tomita, S. Hiura, S. Hagihara and N. Yonezaki, A temporal logic with mean-payoff constraints, in *Formal Methods and Software Engineering*, eds. T. Aoki and K. Taguchi, Lecture Notes in Computer Science, Vol. 7635 (Springer Berlin Heidelberg, 2012) pp. 249–265.

4. D. Giannakopoulou and F. Lerda, From states to transitions: Improving translation of ltl formulae to büchi automata, in *Formal Techniques for Networked and Distributed Systems*, eds. D. A. Peled and M. Y. Vardi, Lecture Notes in Computer Science, Vol. 2529 (Springer Berlin Heidelberg, 2002) pp. 308–326.

5. A. E. B. Salem, A. Duret-Lutz and F. Kordon, Generalized büchi automata versus testing automata for model checking, *Proceedings of the 2nd workshop on Scalable and Usable Model Checking for Petri Nets and other models of Concurrency* **726**, 65 (2011).

6. A. Pnueli and R. Rosner, On the synthesis of a reactive module, in *Proceedings of the 16th ACM SIGPLAN-SIGACT Symposium on Principles of Programming Languages*, (ACM, 1989) pp. 179–190.

7. M. Abadi, L. Lamport and P. Wolper, Realizable and unrealizable specifications of reactive systems, in *Automata, Languages and Programming*, eds. G. Ausiello, M. Dezani-Ciancaglini and S. Della Rocca, Lecture Notes in Computer Science, Vol. 372 (Springer Berlin Heidelberg, 1989) pp. 1–17.

8. A. Bohy, V. Bruyére, E. Filiot and J.-F. Raskin, Synthesis from ltl specifications with mean-payoff objectives, in *Tools and Algorithms for the Construction and Analysis of Systems*, eds. N. Piterman and S. Smolka, Lecture Notes in Computer Science, Vol. 7795 (Springer Berlin Heidelberg, 2013) pp. 169–184.

9. M. Y. Vardi, An automata-theoretic approach to linear temporal logic, in *Logics for Concurrency*, eds. F. Moller and G. Birtwistle, Lecture Notes in Computer Science, Vol. 1043 (Springer Berlin Heidelberg, 1996) pp. 238–266.

10. T. Babiak, M. Křetínský, V. Řehák and J. Strejček, Ltl to büchi automata translation: Fast and more deterministic, in *Tools and Algorithms for the Construction and Analysis of Systems*, eds. C. Flanagan and B. König, Lecture Notes in Computer Science, Vol. 7214 (Springer Berlin Heidelberg, 2012) pp. 95–109.

11. B. Dutertre and L. de Moura, A fast linear-arithmetic solver for dpll(t), in *Computer Aided Verification*, eds. T. Ball and R. B. Jones, Lecture Notes in Computer Science, Vol. 4144 (Springer Berlin Heidelberg, 2006) pp. 81–94.

12. T. Aoshima and N. Yonezaki, Verification of reactive system specifications with outer event conditional formula, in *Principles of Software Evolution, 2000., Proceedings of International Symposium on*, (IEEE, 2000) pp. 189–193.

Appendix A. Sample Specification

In this appendix, we give a parameterized LTL formula and mean-payoff formulae which were used as inputs for some experiments in Sec. 4.

The LTL formula $\psi_{\text{elv}}(n)$ is a functional specification for an n-floor elevator system with a single lift, which is used as an example in Ref. 12. It is given as a conjunction of the following formulae:

$$\mathbf{G}(\bigvee_{1 \le i \le n} Loc_i), \tag{A.1}$$

$$\mathbf{G}(\bigwedge_{1 \le i \le n} (Loc_i \to \bigwedge_{\substack{1 \le j \le n, \\ j \ne i}} \neg Loc_j)), \tag{A.2}$$

$$\mathbf{G}(\bigwedge_{1 \le i \le n} (LocBtn_i \to (\mathbf{F} Loc_i \wedge (Loc_i \mathbf{R} ReqLoc_i)))), \tag{A.3}$$

$$\mathbf{G}(\bigwedge_{1 \le i \le n} ((Loc_i \wedge ReqLoc_i) \to (Open \wedge (Movable \mathbf{R}(Movable \vee Loc_i))))), \tag{A.4}$$

$$\mathbf{G}(\bigwedge_{1 \le i \le n} ((Loc_i \wedge Movable) \to (LocBtn_i \mathbf{R}(LocBtn_i \vee \neg ReqLoc_i)))), \tag{A.5}$$

$$\mathbf{G}(\bigwedge_{1 \le i \le n} ((Loc_i \wedge \neg ReqLoc_i) \to \neg Open)), \tag{A.6}$$

$$\mathbf{G}(Open \to (\neg Open \mathbf{R}(\neg Open \vee \neg Movable))), \tag{A.7}$$

$$\mathbf{G}(\neg Open \to (Open \mathbf{R}(Open \vee Movable))), \tag{A.8}$$

$$\mathbf{G}(\neg Open \to \mathbf{F} OpenTimedOut), \tag{A.9}$$

$$\mathbf{G}((OpenBtn \wedge \neg OpenTimedOut) \to ReqOpen), \tag{A.10}$$

$$\mathbf{G}(OpenTimedOut \to \neg Open), \tag{A.11}$$

$$\mathbf{G}((CloseBtn \wedge \neg ReqOpen) \to \neg Open), \tag{A.12}$$

$$\mathbf{G}((ReqOpen \wedge \neg Movable) \to Open), \tag{A.13}$$

and additional formulae for $n \ge 3$ as follows:

$$\mathbf{G}(\bigwedge_{\substack{1 \le i \le n-2, \\ \max\{3, i+2\} \le j \le n}} ((Loc_i \wedge ReqLoc_j) \to \bigwedge_{i+2 \le k \le j} (Loc_k \mathbf{U} Loc_{k-1}))), \tag{A.14}$$

$$\mathbf{G}(\bigwedge_{\substack{1 \le i \le n-2, \\ \max\{3, i+2\} \le j \le n}} ((Loc_j \wedge ReqLoc_i) \to \bigwedge_{i+2 \le k \le j} (Loc_k \mathbf{U} Loc_{k+1}))). \tag{A.15}$$

The intuitive meanings of atomic propositions in $\varphi_{\text{elv}}(n)$ are, for $1 \le i \le n$, as follows: Loc_i means "the lift is located at i-th floor," $LocBtn_i$ means "a lift-request button is pushed at the i-th floor," $ReqLoc_i$ means "the lift-request at the i-th floor must be served," $Open$ means "a door of the lift is open," $OpenBtn$ means "a door-open button in the lift is pushed," $CloseBtn$ means "a door-close button in the lift is pushed," $ReqOpen$ means "a user is waiting for the door to be opened," $OpenTimedOut$ means "a door-open duration has timed out," and $Movable$ means "the lift is movable."

The mean-payoff formulae $\theta_1, \ldots, \theta_4$ and $\theta_5(n)$ are performance specifications given as the following formulae:

$$\theta_1 = \mathbf{MP}(5 \cdot \mathbf{1}_{Loc_1 \mathbf{U} Loc_2}) \geq 1, \tag{A.16}$$

$$\theta_2 = \overline{\mathbf{MP}}(3 \cdot \mathbf{1}_{Movable} + \mathbf{1}_{Open}) \leq 2, \tag{A.17}$$

$$\theta_3 = \mathbf{MP}(5 \cdot \mathbf{1}_{Movable}) \geq 1, \tag{A.18}$$

$$\theta_4 = \mathbf{MP}(5 \cdot \mathbf{1}_{Loc_1}) \geq 1, \tag{A.19}$$

$$\theta_5(n) = \mathbf{MP}(10 \cdot \mathbf{1}_{ReqLoc_n}) \geq 1. \tag{A.20}$$

Intuitively, θ_1 means "the frequency of satisfying $Loc_1 \mathbf{U} Loc_2$ is bounded below by $1/5$," θ_2 means "the long-run average cost is bounded above by 2, when a movable-state of the lift and an open-state of the door cost 3 and 1 per a step, respectively," θ_3 means "the frequency that the lift is movable is bounded below by $1/5$," θ_4 means "the frequency of keeping the lift at the first floor is bounded below by $1/5$," and $\theta_5(n)$ means "the frequency of pushing the lift-request button at the highest (*i.e.*, n-th) floor is bounded below by $1/10$."

LAZY RPC AND RMI CALCULI

Shota Araki and Shin-ya Nishizaki

*Department of Computer Science, Tokyo Institute of Technology,
Tokyo, 152-8552, Japan
E-mail:nisizaki@cs.titech.ac.jp*

The remote procedure call (RPC) is a widely used technology for programming in distributed computation. Cooper and Wadler proposed the RPC calculus in order to model remote procedure calls. In object-oriented programming languages, the remote method invocation (RMI) is introduced as its variation. RMI calculus, proposed by Matsumoto and Nishizaki, is a formal system based on the sigma calculus which formulates prototype-based object-oriented programming language, incorporated with remote method invocations. Araki and Nishizaki proposed call-by-name evaluation strategies of RMI calculus and of RPC calculus and studied correspondence between the call-by-name evaluation strategies of the RMI and RPC calculi. In this paper, we give call-by-need evaluation strategies to RMI and RPC calculi, which are called lazy RMI and RPC calculi. We show the soundness property of lazy RMI calculus with respect to the lazy RPC calculus.

Keywords: Lambda Calculus; Remort Procedure Call; RPC Calculus; Evaluation Strategy; Call-by-Need Evaluation

1. Introduction

An *evaluation strategy* is a set of rules for evaluating expressions in a programming language, which defines in what order the arguments of a function are evaluated and when they are substituted into the function.

In *call-by-name* evaluation, an actual parameter expression is bound to the corresponding formal parameter variable before it is evaluated. In the lambda calculus, call-by-name evaluation is formulated as follow.

$$\frac{M \Downarrow \lambda x.M' \quad M'\{x \leftarrow N\} \Downarrow V}{(MN) \Downarrow V}$$

$$\overline{x \Downarrow x}, \quad \overline{\lambda x.M \Downarrow \lambda x.M}, \quad \frac{M \Downarrow V}{(xM) \Downarrow (xV)}.$$

Call-by-name evaluation is occasionally preferable to call-by-value evaluation, since if a formal parameter is not used in a function body, then its actual parameter expression is not evaluated.

It is known that call-by-value evaluation is dual to call-by-name with respect to linear negation of Girard's linear logic[1][2][3].

Call-by-need evaluation is a memoized variant of call-by-name: if the actual parameter expression is evaluated, then its resulting value is memoized for subsequent uses. Lazy functional languages such as the programming language Haskell is based on call-by-need evaluation strategy. Call-by-need evaluation was formalized by Ariola et al.[4] as small step semantics. In their formalization, let-expressions enable postponement of actual-parameters' evaluation.

$$(\lambda x.M)N \to \text{let } x = N \text{ in } M,$$
$$\text{let } x = V \text{ in } C[x] \to \text{let } x = V \text{ in } C[V],$$
$$(\text{let } x = L \text{ in } M)N \to \text{let } x = L \text{ in } (MN),$$
$$\text{let } y = (\text{let } x = L \text{ in } M) \text{ in } N \to \text{let } x = L \text{ in } \text{let } y = M \text{ in } N.$$

1.1. *The Call-by-Name RMI Calculi*

The RMI calculus was proposed by Matsumoto and Nishizaki[5] in order to formalize the remote message invocation in the framework of ς-calculus, which is one of the fragments of the object calculus[6]. In the RMI calculus, locations are introduced into the syntax and they are attached to each self parameter binding. We define a calculus ςrmi^{let}-calculus extended with let-binding, which is utilized in order to translate the λrpc-calculus into the RMI calculus. If we restrict the usage of let-bindings, the calculus is considered as the ςrmi-calculus.

Araki and Nishizaki[7] proposed call-by-name evaluation strategy of the RMI calculus.

Definition 1.1 (Terms of ςrmi^{CBN}-calculi). Terms *of* ςrmi^{CBN} *calculus are defined inductively by the following grammar:*

$a, b, c ::=$		*term*
	x	*variable*
	$[l_i = \varsigma(m_i, x_i)b_i]^{i \in 1..n}$	*object*
	$a.l$	*method invocation*
	$a.l \Leftarrow \varsigma(m, x)b$	*method override*
	$\text{let}^{*m} \ x = v.l \text{ in } b$	*let-binding with location*
	$\text{eval}^m(a)$	*evaluation with location,*

where v is a value, *which is either a variable or an object.*

In a method override $a.l \Leftarrow \varsigma(m, x)b$, if a self parameter x does not appear in its body b, we write it as $a.l :=^m b$. Similarly, if a self parameter x_i does not appear in an entry $l_i = \varsigma(m_i, x_i)b_i$ of an object, we write it as $l_i =^{m_i} b_i$.

Before giving call-by-name evaluation to the RMI calculus, we define values of the calculus.

Definition 1.2 (Values of the ςrmi^{CBN}-calculus). *A value of the ςrmi^{CBN}-calculus is given by either a variable x or an object $[l_i = \varsigma(m_i, x_i)b_i]^{i \in 1..n}$.*

Definition 1.3 (Operational Semantics of ςrmi^{CBN}).
The operational semantics of the ςrmi^{CBN}-calculus is given by the following rules.

$$\frac{}{v \Downarrow_m^{\text{CBN}} v} \text{ Value}$$

$$\frac{a \Downarrow_m^{\text{CBV}} o \quad b_j\{x_j \leftarrow o\} \Downarrow_{m_j}^{\text{CBV}} v}{a.l_j \Downarrow_m^{\text{CBV}} v} \text{ Select}$$

$$\frac{a \Downarrow_m^{\text{CBN}} o}{a.l_j \Leftarrow \varsigma(m', x)b \Downarrow_m^{\text{CBN}} \left[l_j = \varsigma(m', x)b, \ l_i = \varsigma(m_i, x_i)b_i^{i \in 1..n - \{j\}}\right]} \text{ Override}$$

$$\frac{b\{x \leftarrow \text{eval}^{m_j}(b_j\{x_j \leftarrow o\})\} \Downarrow_m^{\text{CBN}} v}{\text{let}^{*m} \ x = o.l_j \text{ in } b \Downarrow_m^{\text{CBV}} v} \text{ Let}$$

$$\frac{a \Downarrow_n^{\text{CBN}} v}{\text{eval}^n(a) \Downarrow_v^{\text{CBN}}} \text{ Eval}$$

1.2. *Research Purpose*

In the previous works[5,7], Nishizaki studied the relationship between the RPC and RMI calculi. Specifically, in the work[5], we show the correspondence between these two calculi with respect to call-by-value evaluation strategy; in the work[7], with respect to call-by-name evaluation strategy.

In this paper, we propose call-by-need evaluation strategy for the RPC and RMI calculi and *prove the soundness of these calculi with respect to a translation between these calculi.*

2. Call-by-Need RPC Calculus

We formulate a call-by-need RPC calculus, $\lambda_{\mathrm{rpc}}^{\mathrm{Need}}$-calculus, in the style of Ariola et al.[4], such as small-step semantics. We first define a syntax of the $\lambda_{\mathrm{rpc}}^{\mathrm{Need}}$-calculus.

Definition 2.1 (locations, terms, values and results of $\lambda_{\mathrm{rpc}}^{\mathrm{Need}}$-calculus). *We define* locations, terms, values, *and* results *by the following grammar.*

$$
\begin{aligned}
a, b &::= \mathsf{c} \mid \mathsf{s} && \textit{locations} \\
M, N &::= x \mid (\lambda^a x.M) \mid (M\ N) && \textit{terms} \\
&\quad \mid (\mathsf{let}^a\ x = M \text{ in } N) \mid (\mathsf{eval}^a M) \\
V &::= (\lambda^a x.M) && \textit{value} \\
A &::= V \mid (\mathsf{let}^a\ x = M \text{ in } A) && \textit{result}
\end{aligned}
$$

Next, we define a notion of *evaluation context* in order to indicate a location to be evaluated.

Definition 2.2 (Evaluation Context of $\lambda_{\mathrm{rpc}}^{\mathrm{Need}}$-calculus). *We define* evaluation contexts *of $\lambda_{\mathrm{rpc}}^{\mathrm{Need}}$ inductively by the following grammar:*

$$
\begin{aligned}
E[\ ] ::=\ & [\ ] \mid (E[\ ]\ M) \\
& \mid (\mathsf{let}^a\ x = E_1[\ ] \text{ in } E_2[\ ]) \\
& \mid (\mathsf{let}^a\ x = M \text{ in } E[\ ]) \\
& \mid (\mathsf{eval}^a E[\ ])
\end{aligned}
$$

Example 2.1. If you are given a term

A term $(\mathsf{let}^s\ x = (\mathsf{eval}^c(\lambda^c y.y)(\lambda^c z.z))$ in $(x\ x))$ can be written as $(\mathsf{let}^s\ x = E_1[(\lambda^c y.y)(\lambda^c z.z)]$ in $E_2[x])$, where $E_1[\ ]$ and $E_2[\ ]$ are supposed to be $(\mathsf{eval}^c[\ ])$ and $([\ ]\ x)$, respectively.

A call-by-need evaluation strategy is defined as small step semantics using the evaluation context.

Definition 2.3 (Call-by-Need Reduction of $\lambda_{\mathrm{rpc}}^{\mathrm{Need}}$-calculus). *A ternary relation $M \to_a N$ among terms M, N and a location a, called* call-by-need reduction *relation, is defined by the following rules.*

$$(\lambda^a x.M)N \to_b \text{let}^a\ x = (\text{eval}^b N)\ \text{in}\ M \qquad \textbf{Beta}$$

$$\text{let}^a\ x = V\ \text{in}\ E[x] \to_a \text{let}^a\ x = V\ \text{in}\ E[V] \qquad \textbf{Deref}$$

$$(\text{let}^a\ x = M\ \text{in}\ A)N \to_a \text{let}^a\ x = M\ \text{in}\ (AN) \qquad \textbf{Lift}$$

$$\text{let}^a\ x = (\text{let}^b\ y = M\ \text{in}\ A)\ \text{in}\ E[x] \to_a \text{let}^b\ y = M\ \text{in}$$
$$(\text{let}^a\ x = A\ \text{in}\ E[x]) \qquad \textbf{Assoc}$$

$$(\text{eval}^a A) \to_a A. \qquad \textbf{Eval}$$

$$\frac{M \to_b M'}{(MN) \to_b (M'N),} \qquad \frac{M \to_a M'}{(\text{eval}^a M) \to_b (\text{eval}^a M'),}$$

$$\frac{M \to_b M'}{(\text{let}^a\ x = M\ \text{in}\ E[x]) \to_b (\text{let}^a\ x = M'\ \text{in}\ E[x]),}$$

$$\frac{N \to_a N'}{(\text{let}^a\ x = M\ \text{in}\ N) \to_b (\text{let}^a\ x = M\ \text{in}\ N'),}$$

A sequence $M \to_{m_1} M_1 \to_{m_2} \cdots \to_{m_n} M_n$ (where $m_1, \ldots, m_n$ are locations) is abbreviated as $M \to_{m_1, m_2, \ldots, m_n} M_n$. The suffix is sometimes omitted, such as $M \xrightarrow{*} M'$.

Example 2.2 (Reduction Sequence). *The following is an example of evaluation sequence, in which you can take arbitrary locations as* $m, m_1, \ldots, m_4.$

$$(\lambda^c x.xx)(\lambda^s y.y)$$
$$\to_m \text{let}^c\ x = \text{eval}^m(\lambda^s y.y)\ \text{in}\ (xx)$$
$$\to_{m_1} \text{let}^c\ x = \lambda^s y.y\ \text{in}\ (xx)$$
$$\quad where\ \text{eval}^m(\lambda^s y.y) \to_c \lambda^s y.y,$$
$$\to_c \text{let}^c\ x = \lambda^s y.y\ \text{in}\ ((\lambda^s y.y)x)$$
$$\to_{m_2} \text{let}^c\ x = \lambda^s y.y\ \text{in}\ (\text{let}^s\ y = (\text{eval}^c x)\ \text{in}\ y)$$
$$\quad where\ ((\lambda^s y.y)x) \to_c (\text{let}^s\ y = (\text{eval}^c x)\ \text{in}\ y)$$
$$\to_c \text{let}^c\ x = \lambda^s y.y\ \text{in}\ (\text{let}^s\ y = (\text{eval}^c(\lambda^s y.y))\ \text{in}\ y)$$
$$\to_{m_3} \text{let}^c\ x = \lambda^s y.y\ \text{in}\ (\text{let}^s\ y = (\lambda^s y.y)\ \text{in}\ y)$$
$$\quad where\ (\text{eval}^c(\lambda^s y.y)) \to_c (\lambda^s y.y)$$
$$\to_{m_4} \text{let}^c\ x = \lambda^s y.y\ \text{in}\ (\text{let}^s\ y = (\lambda^s y.y)\ \text{in}\ (\lambda^s y.y))$$
$$\quad where\ (\text{let}^s\ y = (\lambda^s y.y)\ \text{in}\ y) \to_s (\text{let}^s\ y = (\lambda^s y.y)\ \text{in}\ (\lambda^s y.y)).$$

3. Call-by-Need RMI Calculus

Next, we formulate a call-by-need RMI calculus, $\varsigma\text{rmi}^{\text{Need}}$–calculus, based on $\varsigma\text{rmi}^{\text{CBV}}$- and $\varsigma\text{rmi}^{\text{CBN}}$-calculi[5][7][8].

Definition 3.1 (locations, terms, values and results of $\varsigma\text{rmi}^{\text{Need}}$-calculus).
We define location, terms, values, and results by the following grammar.

$$
\begin{aligned}
m, n &::= \textsf{c} \mid \textsf{s} &&\textit{locations}\\
a, b &::= &&\textit{terms}\\
&\quad x \mid [l_i = \varsigma(m_i, x_i)b_i^{i\in 1..n}]\\
&\quad \mid a.l \mid a.l \Leftarrow \varsigma(m, x)b\\
&\quad \mid (\textsf{let}^{*m}\ x = a.l\ \textsf{in}\ b)\\
&\quad \mid (\textsf{let}^m\ x = a\ \textsf{in}\ b)\\
&\quad \mid \textsf{eval}^m(a)\\
v &::= [l_i = \varsigma(m_i, x_i)b_i^{i\in 1..n}] \qquad f ::= v \mid (\textsf{let}^m\ x = a\ \textsf{in}\ f) \quad \textit{results}
\end{aligned}
$$

We give evaluation contexts to the $\varsigma\text{rmi}^{\text{Need}}$-calculus.

Definition 3.2 (Evaluation context of $\varsigma\text{rmi}^{\text{Need}}$-calculus). *We define evaluation contexts of $\varsigma\text{rmi}^{\text{Need}}$-calculus by the following grammar.*

$$
\begin{aligned}
e[\,] ::=&\ [\,]\\
&\mid e[\,].l\\
&\mid e[\,].l \Leftarrow \varsigma(m, x)b\\
&\mid \textsf{let}^m\ x = e[\,]\ \textsf{in}\ e'[x]\\
&\mid \textsf{let}^m\ x = a\ \textsf{in}\ e[\,]\\
&\mid \textsf{eval}^m(e[\,])
\end{aligned}
$$

Based on the evaluation contexts, we can define a redution relation of $\varsigma\text{rmi}^{\text{Need}}$-calculus.

Definition 3.3 (Call-by-Need Reduction of $\varsigma\text{rmi}^{\text{Need}}$-calculus).
We define a reduction relation of the $\varsigma\text{rmi}^{\text{Need}}$-calculus among terms M, N and a location a by the following rules.

$$o.l_j \rightarrow_n \mathsf{eval}^{m_j}(b_j\{x_j \leftarrow o\}) \qquad\qquad \textbf{Select}$$

$$o.l_j \Leftarrow \varsigma(m,y)b \rightarrow_n \left[l_j = \varsigma(m,y)b,\right.$$

$$\left. l_i = \varsigma(m_i,x_i)b_i^{i\in 1..n-\{j\}}\right] \qquad\qquad \textbf{Update}$$

$$(\mathsf{let}^{*m}\ x = o.l_j\ \mathsf{in}\ a) \rightarrow_m \mathsf{let}^m\ x = \mathsf{eval}^{m_j}(b_j\{x_j \leftarrow o\})\ \mathsf{in}\ a \qquad \textbf{Let}^*$$

$$(\mathsf{let}^m\ x = v\ \mathsf{in}\ e[x]) \rightarrow_m (\mathsf{let}^m\ x = v\ \mathsf{in}\ e[v]) \qquad\qquad \textbf{Deref}$$

$$(\mathsf{let}^m\ x = (\mathsf{let}^n\ y = a\ \mathsf{in}\ f) \rightarrow_m (\mathsf{let}^n\ x = a \qquad\qquad \textbf{Assoc}$$
$$\mathsf{in}\ e[x]) \qquad \mathsf{in}\ (\mathsf{let}^m\ x = f\ \mathsf{in}\ e[x]))$$

The expression $b_j\{x_j \leftarrow o\}$ means a substitution of o for x_j in b_j. In the style of lambda calculus, it could be written as $b_j[x_j := o]$.

$$\frac{a \rightarrow_n a'}{a.l \rightarrow_n a'.l} \qquad \frac{a \rightarrow_n a'}{a.l_j \Leftarrow \varsigma(m,x)b \rightarrow_n a'.l_j \Leftarrow \varsigma(m,x)b}$$

$$\frac{a \rightarrow_m a'}{\mathsf{let}^m\ x = a\ \mathsf{in}\ e[x] \rightarrow_n \mathsf{let}^m\ x = a'\ \mathsf{in}\ e[x]}$$

$$\frac{b \rightarrow_m b'}{\mathsf{let}^m\ x = a\ \mathsf{in}\ b \rightarrow_n \mathsf{let}^m\ x = a\ \mathsf{in}\ b'}$$

$$\frac{a \rightarrow_m a'}{\mathsf{eval}^m(a) \rightarrow_n \mathsf{eval}^m(a')}$$

Example 3.1 (Example of Reduction Sequence). *Let $m_1, \ldots, m_5$ be arbitrary locations.*

$$([arg =^s 0,\ getArg - \varsigma(s,x)\ \mathsf{let}^{*s}\ x - x.arg\ \mathsf{in}\ x].arg :=^c 5).getArg$$

$$\rightarrow_{m_1} ([arg =^c 5,\ getArg = \varsigma(s,x)\ \mathsf{let}^{*s}\ x = x.arg\ \mathsf{in}\ x]).getArg$$

$$\rightarrow_{m_2} \mathsf{eval}^s(\mathsf{let}^{*s}\ x = [arg =^c 5,\ getArg = \varsigma(s,x)\ \mathsf{let}^{*s}\ x = x.arg\ \mathsf{in}\ x].arg\ \mathsf{in}\ x)$$

$$\rightarrow_{m_3} \mathsf{eval}^s(\mathsf{let}^{*s}\ x = 5\ \mathsf{in}\ x)$$

$$where\ \mathsf{let}^{*s}\ x = [arg =^c 5,\ \cdots].arg\ \mathsf{in}\ x \rightarrow_s \mathsf{let}^{*s}\ x = 5\ \mathsf{in}\ x$$

$$\rightarrow_{m_4} \mathsf{eval}^s(\mathsf{let}^{*s}\ x = 5\ \mathsf{in}\ 5)$$

$$where\ \mathsf{let}^{*s}\ x = 5\ \mathsf{in}\ x \rightarrow_s \mathsf{let}^{*s}\ x = 5\ \mathsf{in}\ 5$$

$$\rightarrow_{m_5} \mathsf{let}^{*s}\ x = 5\ \mathsf{in}\ 5$$

4. Translation of Lazy RMI Calculus into Lazy RPC Calculus

In this section, we give a translation of lazy RMI calculus $\varsigma\text{rmi}^{\text{Need}}$ into lazy RPC calculus $\lambda_{\text{rpc}}^{\text{Need}}$ and show soundness theorem of the $\varsigma\text{rmi}^{\text{Need}}$-calculus with respect to the $\lambda_{\text{rpc}}^{\text{Need}}$-calculus.

Definition 4.1 (Term Translation). *We define a mapping* $\langle M \rangle_m^{need}$, *called a term transformation, of a term M of $\lambda_{\text{rpc}}^{\text{Need}}$-calculus and a location m into a term of $\varsigma\text{rmi}^{\text{Need}}$-calculus, inductively by the following equations.*

$$\langle x \rangle_m^{need} = [\,]$$
$$\langle (\text{let}^n \ x = N \ \text{in} \ M) \rangle_m^{need} = (\text{let}^n \ x = \langle N \rangle_n^{need} \ \text{in} \ \langle M \rangle_n^{need})$$
$$\langle (MN) \rangle_m^{need} = (\langle M \rangle_m^{need}.arg :=^m \langle N \rangle_m^{need}).val$$
$$\langle \text{eval}^n(M) \rangle_m^{need} = \text{eval}^n(\langle M \rangle_n^{need})$$
$$\langle (\lambda^n x.M) \rangle_m^{need} = [arg = \varsigma(n,x)x.arg, \ val = \varsigma(n,x)(\text{let}^{*n} \ x = x.arg \ \text{in} \ \langle M \rangle_n^{need}]$$

Definition 4.2 (Context Translation). *We define a mapping* $\langle E[\,] \rangle_m^e$, *called a context transformation, of an evaluation context $E[\,]$ of $\lambda_{\text{rpc}}^{\text{Need}}$-calculus and a location m into an evaluation context of $\varsigma\text{rmi}^{\text{Need}}$-calculus, inductively by the following equations.*

$$\langle [\,] \rangle_m^e = [\,]$$
$$\langle (E[\,] \ M) \rangle_m^e = (\langle E[\,] \rangle_m^e.arg :=^m \langle M \rangle_m^{need}).val$$
$$\langle (\text{let}^n \ x = E[\,] \ \text{in} \ E'[x]) \rangle_m^e = (\text{let}^n \ x = \langle E[\,] \rangle_n^e \ \text{in} \ \langle E'[x] \rangle_n^{need})$$
$$\langle (\text{let}^n \ x = M \ \text{in} \ E[\,]) \rangle_m^e = (\text{let}^n \ x = \langle M \rangle_n^{need} \ \text{in} \ \langle E[\,] \rangle_n^e)$$
$$\langle \text{eval}^n(E[\,]) \rangle_m^e = \text{eval}^n(\langle E[\,] \rangle_n^e)$$

The following proposition is directly derived from the definition of the transformation $\langle (-) \rangle_{(-)}^{need}$.

Proposition 4.1. *For a variable x and a value V, it holds that* $\langle x \rangle_m^{need} = \langle x \rangle_n^{need}$ *and* $\langle V \rangle_m^{need} = \langle V \rangle_n^{need}$.

Lemma 4.1 (Context Lemma). *For an evaluation context $E[\,]$ of the*

$\lambda_{\text{rpc}}^{\text{Need}}$-*calculus, a variable* x, *a value* V *and a location* m, *it holds that*

$$e\left[\langle x\rangle_n^{need}\right] = \langle E[x]\rangle_m^{need}$$

and

$$e\left[\langle V\rangle_n^{need}\right] = \langle E[V]\rangle_m^{need}.$$

where $e[\ ] \overset{def}{=} \langle E[\ ]\rangle_m^e$.

Proof. We prove this lemma by induction on structure of the evaluation context $E[\ ]$.

Case: $E[\ ]$ is the empty context $[\ ]$. This case is trivial.

Case: $E[\ ] = (E'[\ ]\ M)$. Let $e'[\ ]$ be $\langle E'[\ ]\rangle_m^e$. We have

$$
\begin{aligned}
e[\ ] &= \langle (E'[\ ]\ M)\rangle_m^e\\
&= (\langle E'[\ ]\rangle_m^e).arg :=^m \langle M\rangle_m^{need}).val\\
&= (e'[\ ].arg :=^m \langle M\rangle_m^{need}).val.
\end{aligned}
$$

$$
\begin{aligned}
e[\langle V\rangle_n^{need}] &= (e'[\langle V\rangle_n^{need}].arg :=^m \langle M\rangle_m^{need}).val\\
&= (\langle E'[V]\rangle_m^{need}.arg :=^m \langle M\rangle_m^{need}).val\\
&\quad \text{by the induction hypothesis}\\
&= \langle (E'[V]\ M)\rangle_m^{need}\\
&= \langle E[V]\rangle_m^{need}.
\end{aligned}
$$

Case: $E[\ ] = (\text{let}^l\ x = E'[\ ]\ \text{in}\ E''[x])$. Let $e'[\ ]$ be $\langle E'[\ ]\rangle_m^e$. We have

$$
\begin{aligned}
e[\ ] &= \langle E[\ ]\rangle_m^e\\
&= \langle \text{let}^l\ x = E'[\ ]\ \text{in}\ E''[x]\rangle_m^e\\
&= \text{let}^l\ x = \langle E'[\ ]\rangle_l^e\ \text{in}\ \langle E''[x]\rangle_l^{need}\\
&= \text{let}^l\ x = e'[\ ]\ \text{in}\ \langle E''[x]\rangle_l^{need}.
\end{aligned}
$$

Therefore, we have

$$e[\langle V \rangle_n^{need}]$$
$$= \text{let}^l \; x = e'[\langle V \rangle_n^{need}] \text{ in } \langle E''[x] \rangle_l^{need}$$
$$= \text{let}^l \; x = \langle E'[V] \rangle_l^{need} \text{ in } \langle E''[x] \rangle_l^{need}$$
$$\text{by the induction hypothesis,}$$
$$= \langle \text{let}^l \; x = E'[V] \text{ in } E''[x] \rangle_l^{need}$$
$$= \langle E[V] \rangle_l^{need}.$$

Case: $E[\;] = (\text{let}^l \; x = M \text{ in } E'[\;])$. Let $e'[\;]$ be $\langle E'[\;] \rangle_m^e$. We have

$$e[\;] = \langle E[\;] \rangle_m^e$$
$$= \langle \text{let}^l \; x = m \text{ in } E'[\;] \rangle_m^e$$
$$= \text{let}^l \; x = \langle M \rangle_l^e \text{ in } \langle E'[\;] \rangle_l^{need}$$
$$= \text{let}^l \; x = \langle M \rangle_l^e \text{ in } e'[\;].$$

Therefore, we have

$$e[\langle V \rangle_n^{need}]$$
$$= \text{let}^l \; x = \langle M \rangle_l^{need} \text{ in } e'[\langle V \rangle_n^{need}]$$
$$= \text{let}^l \; x = \langle M \rangle_l^{need} \text{ in } \langle E'[V] \rangle_l^{need}$$
$$\text{by the induction hypothesis,}$$
$$= \langle \text{let}^l \; x = M \text{ in } E'[\;] \rangle_l^{need}$$
$$= \langle E[V] \rangle_l^{need}.$$

Case: $E[\;] = \text{eval}^l(E'[\;])$. Let $e'[\;]$ be $\langle E'[\;] \rangle_m^e$. We have

$$e[\;] = \langle E[\;] \rangle_m^e$$
$$= \langle \text{eval}^l(E'[\;]) \rangle_m^e$$
$$= \text{eval}^l(\langle E'[\;] \rangle_m^e)$$
$$= \text{eval}^l(e'[\;]).$$

Therefore, we have

$$e[\langle V \rangle_n^{need}]$$
$$= \mathsf{eval}^l(e'[\langle V \rangle_n^{need}])$$
$$= \mathsf{eval}^l(\langle E'[V] \rangle_l^{need})$$
$$= \langle \mathsf{eval}^l(E'[V]) \rangle_m^{need}$$
$$= \langle E[V] \rangle_m^{need}$$

$\square$

Next, we show soundness of the translations $\langle M \rangle_m^{need}$ and $\langle E[\ ] \rangle_m^e$ with respect to the reductions.

Theorem 4.1 (Soundness of Translation). *For terms M and M' of $\lambda_{\mathrm{rpc}}^{\mathrm{Need}}$-calculus and a location m, if $M \to_m M'$ and $\langle M \rangle_m^{need}$ and $\langle M' \rangle_m^{need}$ are terminating, then $\langle M \rangle_m^{need}$ and $\langle M' \rangle_m^{need}$ have the same result, that is, there exists a result f of $\varsigma\mathrm{rmi}^{\mathrm{Need}}$-calculus satisfying that $\langle M \rangle_m^{need} \overset{*}{\to} f$ and $\langle M' \rangle_m^{need} \overset{*}{\to} f$.*

Proof. We prove this theorem by induction on the structure of the $\lambda_{\mathrm{rpc}}^{\mathrm{Need}}$-calculus' reduction. The step cases are trivial and we show the base cases in the following.

Case: $((\lambda^n x.M)N) \to_m (\mathsf{let}^n\ x = \mathsf{eval}^m(N)\ \mathsf{in}\ M)$.

$$\langle ((\lambda^n x.M)N) \rangle_m^{need}$$
$$= \left(\langle \lambda^n x.M \rangle_m^{need}.arg :=^m \langle N \rangle_m^{need} \right).val$$
$$= ([arg = \varsigma(n,x)x.arg,$$
$$val = \varsigma(n,x)(\mathsf{let}^{*n}\ x = x.arg\ \mathsf{in}\ \langle M \rangle_n^{need})]$$
$$.arg :=^m \langle N \rangle_m^{need}).val$$

$$\rightarrow_m \; ([arg =^m \langle N \rangle_m^{need},$$
$$val = \varsigma(n,x)(\mathsf{let}^{*n} \; x = x.arg \; \mathsf{in} \; \langle M \rangle_n^{need})]$$
$$.arg :=^m \langle N \rangle_m^{need}).val$$

$$\rightarrow_m \mathsf{eval}^n(\mathsf{let}^{*n} \; x = [arg =^m \langle N \rangle_m^{need},$$
$$val = \varsigma(n,x)$$
$$\mathsf{let}^{*n} \; x = x.arg \; \mathsf{in} \; \langle M \rangle_n^{need}]$$
$$.arg \; \mathsf{in} \; \langle M \rangle_n^{need})$$

$$\rightarrow_n \mathsf{eval}^n(\mathsf{let}^n \; x = \mathsf{eval}^m(\langle N \rangle_m^{need}) \; \mathsf{in} \; \langle M \rangle_n^{need})$$

$$\xrightarrow{*} \; \mathsf{eval}^n(f)$$

$$\rightarrow_m f$$

where we suppose that $(\mathsf{let}^n \; x = \mathsf{eval}^m(\langle N \rangle_m^{need}) \; \mathsf{in} \; \langle M \rangle_n^{need}) \xrightarrow{*} f$.
On the other hand,

$$\langle \mathsf{let}^n \; x = \mathsf{eval}^m(N) \; \mathsf{in} \; M \rangle_m^{need}$$
$$= \mathsf{let}^n \; x = \langle \mathsf{eval}^m(N) \rangle_n^{need} \; \mathsf{in} \; \langle M \rangle_n^{need}$$
$$= \mathsf{let}^n \; x = \mathsf{eval}^m(\langle N \rangle_n^{need}) \; \mathsf{in} \; \langle M \rangle_n^{need}$$
$$\xrightarrow{*} f$$

Case: $(\mathsf{let}^m \; x = V \; \mathsf{in} \; E[x]) \rightarrow_m (\mathsf{let}^m \; x = V \; \mathsf{in} \; E[V])$.
By the context lemma, if we let $e[\;]$ be $\langle E[\;] \rangle_m^e$, then

$$e[x] = e[\langle x \rangle_m^{need}] = \langle E[x] \rangle_m^{need}$$

and

$$e[\langle V \rangle_m^{need}] = \langle E[V] \rangle_m^{need}.$$

Then, we have

$$\langle \mathsf{let}^m \; x = V \; \mathsf{in} \; E[x] \rangle_m^{need}$$
$$= \mathsf{let}^m \; x = \langle V \rangle_m^{need} \; \mathsf{in} \; \langle E[x] \rangle_m^{need}$$
$$= \mathsf{let}^m \; x = \langle V \rangle_m^{need} \; \mathsf{in} \; e[x]$$
$$\rightarrow_m \mathsf{let}^m \; x = \langle V \rangle_m^{need} \; \mathsf{in} \; e[\langle V \rangle_m^{need}]$$
$$= \mathsf{let}^m \; x = \langle V \rangle_m^{need} \; \mathsf{in} \; e[x]$$
$$\rightarrow_m \mathsf{let}^m \; x = \langle V \rangle_m^{need} \; \mathsf{in} \; \langle E[V] \rangle_m^{need},$$

since $\langle V \rangle_m^{need}$ is a value of the $\varsigma\mathrm{rmi}^{\mathrm{Need}}$-calculus.

On the other hand,

$$\langle \mathsf{let}^n \ x = V \ \mathsf{in} \ E[V] \rangle_m^{need} = \mathsf{let}^n \ x = \langle V \rangle_m^{need} \ \mathsf{in} \ \langle E[V] \rangle_m^{need}.$$

Hence, we have

$$\langle \mathsf{let}^m \ x = V \ \mathsf{in} \ E[x] \rangle_m^{need} \xrightarrow{*}_m \langle \mathsf{let}^n \ x = V \ \mathsf{in} \ E[V] \rangle_m^{need} \xrightarrow{*}_m f.$$

Case: $((\mathsf{let}^m \ x = M \ \mathsf{in} \ A) \ N) \to_m (\mathsf{let}^m \ x = M \ \mathsf{in} \ (A \ N))$.

By definition of the translation, for a result A of $\lambda_{\mathrm{rpc}}^{\mathrm{Need}}$, $\langle A \rangle_m^{need}$ is a result of $\varsigma\mathrm{rmi}^{\mathrm{Need}}$. Hence,

$$\langle (\mathsf{let}^m \ x = M \ \mathsf{in} \ A) N \rangle_m^{need}$$
$$= (\langle \mathsf{let}^m \ x = M \ \mathsf{in} \ A \rangle_m^{need}.arg :=^m \langle N \rangle_m^{need}).val$$
$$= ((\mathsf{let}^m \ x = \langle M \rangle_m^{need} \ \mathsf{in} \ \langle A \rangle_m^{need}).arg :=^m \langle N \rangle_m^{need}).val$$
$$\to_m \mathsf{let}^m \ x = \langle M \rangle_m^{need} \ \mathsf{in} \ (\langle A \rangle_m^{need}.arg :=^m \langle N \rangle_m^{need}).val.$$

On the other hand,

$$\langle \mathsf{let}^m \ x = M \ \mathsf{in} \ (A \ N) \rangle_m^{need}$$
$$= \mathsf{let}^m \ x = \langle M \rangle_m^{need} \ \mathsf{in} \ \langle (A \ N) \rangle_m^{need}$$
$$= \mathsf{let}^m \ x = \langle M \rangle_m^{need} \ \mathsf{in} \ (\langle A \rangle_m^{need}.arg :=^m \langle N \rangle_m^{need}).val.$$

Accordingly, we know

$$\langle (\mathsf{let}^m \ x = M \ \mathsf{in} \ A) N \rangle_m^{need} \to_m \langle \mathsf{let}^m \ x = M \ \mathsf{in} \ (A \ N) \rangle_m^{need}.$$

Case: $(\mathsf{let}^m \ x = (\mathsf{let}^n \ y = M \ \mathsf{in} \ A) \ \mathsf{in} \ E[x]) \to_m (\mathsf{let}^n \ y = M \ \mathsf{in} \ (\mathsf{let}^m \ x = A \ \mathsf{in} \ E[x]))$.

$$\langle \mathsf{let}^m \ x = (\mathsf{let}^n \ y = M \ \mathsf{in} \ A) \ \mathsf{in} \ E[x] \rangle_m^{need}$$
$$= \mathsf{let}^m \ x = \langle \mathsf{let}^n \ y = M \ \mathsf{in} \ A \rangle_m^{need} \ \mathsf{in} \ \langle E[x] \rangle_m^{need}$$
$$= \mathsf{let}^m \ x = (\mathsf{let}^n \ y = \langle M \rangle_n^{need} \ \mathsf{in} \ \langle A \rangle_n^{need}) \ \mathsf{in} \ \langle E[x] \rangle_m^{need}$$
$$\to_m \mathsf{let}^n \ y = \langle M \rangle_n^{need} \ \mathsf{in} \ (\mathsf{let}^m \ x = \langle A \rangle_n^{need} \ \mathsf{in} \ \langle E[x] \rangle_m^{need}).$$

On the other hand,

$$\langle (\mathsf{let}^n \ y = M \ \mathsf{in} \ (\mathsf{let}^m \ x = A \ \mathsf{in} \ E[x])) \rangle_m^{need}$$
$$= \mathsf{let}^n \ y = \langle M \rangle_n^{need} \ \mathsf{in} \ \langle \mathsf{let}^m \ x = A \ \mathsf{in} \ E[x] \rangle_n^{need}$$
$$= \mathsf{let}^n \ y = \langle M \rangle_n^{need} \ \mathsf{in} \ (\mathsf{let}^m \ x = \langle A \rangle_m^{need} \ \mathsf{in} \ \langle E[x] \rangle_m^{need}).$$

Since $\langle A \rangle_m^{need} = \langle A \rangle_n^{need}$,

$$\langle \mathsf{let}^m \ x = (\mathsf{let}^n \ y = M \ \mathsf{in} \ A) \ \mathsf{in} \ E[x] \rangle_m^{need}$$
$$\rightarrow_m \langle (\mathsf{let}^n \ y = M \ \mathsf{in} \ (\mathsf{let}^m \ x = A \ \mathsf{in} \ E[x]))) \rangle_m^{need}.$$

Case: $\mathsf{eval}^n(A) \rightarrow_m A$.

$$\langle \mathsf{eval}^n(A) \rangle_m^{need} = \mathsf{eval}^n(\langle A \rangle_n^{need})$$
$$\rightarrow_m \langle A \rangle_n^{need}$$
$$= \langle A \rangle_m^{need}.$$

$\square$

5. Conclusions

We proposed a call-by-need RPC and RMI calculi, $\lambda_{\mathrm{rpc}}^{\mathrm{Need}}$ and $\varsigma\mathrm{rmi}^{\mathrm{Need}}$, respectively and give a translation of the call-by-need RMI calculus into the call-by-need RPC calculus. We prove the soundness theorem of the call-by-need RMI calculus with respect to the translation. It is not intuitive that the evaluation strategy of the RMI calculus is call-by-need. Giving the translation, the call-by-need evaluation in the functional programming is clearly related to the RMI calculus' evaluation.

One direction of our future research is implementation of the call-by-need RPC and RMI calculi. A lot of researchers have studied implementation of lazy functional programming language compilers and interpreters for many years[9].

References

1. P. Wadler, Call-by-value is dual to call-by-name – reloaded, in *Proceedings of the 16th RTA 2005*, (Springer-Verlag Berlin Heidelberg, 2005).
2. S. Nishizaki, Programs with continuations and linear logic, *Science of Computer Programming* **21**, 165 (1993).
3. J.-Y. Girard, Linear logic, *Theoretical Computer Science* **50**, 1 (1987).
4. Z. M. Ariola, J. Maraist, M. Odersky, M. Felleisen and P. Wadler, The call-by-need lambda calculus, in *Proceedings of the 22nd ACM SIGPLAN-SIGACT symposium on Principles of programming languages*, (ACM Press, 1995).
5. S. Matsumoto and S. Nishizaki, An object calculus with remote method invocation, *Proceedings of the Second Workshop on Computation: Theory and Practice, WCTP2012, Proceedings in Information and Communication Technology* **7**, 34 (2013).

6. M. Abadi and L. Cardelli, *A Theory of Objects* (Springer-Verlag,Berlin, 1996).
7. S. Araki and S. Nishizaki, Call-by-name evaluation of rpc and rmi calculi, *Proceedings of the Third Workshop on Computation: Theory and Practice, WCTP2013, Proceedings in Information and Communication Technology* (2014).
8. S. Araki and Shin-yaj Nishizaki, On lazy evaluation of rmi calculus (2014).
9. S. P. Jones, *The Implementation of Functional Programming Languages* (Prentice Hall, 1987).

LEARNING BETTER STRATEGIES WITH A COMBINATION OF COMPLEMENTARY REINFORCEMENT LEARNING ALGORITHMS

Wataru Fujita*, Koichi Moriyama[†]*, Ken-ichi Fukui[†]* and Masayuki Numao[†]*

*Graduate School of Information Science and Technology, Osaka University
[†] The Institute of Scientific and Industrial Research, Osaka University
8-1, Mihogaoka, Ibaraki, Osaka, 567-0047, Japan
Tel.: +81-6-6879-8426   Fax: +81-6-6879-8428
E-mail: {fujita, koichi, fukui, numao}@ai.sanken.osaka-u.ac.jp

People engage in a variety of interaction in the society. To study the interaction, we see it as a game and people as agents equipped with reinforcement learning algorithms. However, existing algorithms have strong and weak points when dealing with games. In this work, we combined two complementary reinforcement learning algorithms to overcome the weakness. We constructed an algorithm that maximizes payoffs in various games. Our proposed algorithm combined two famous reinforcement algorithms, i.e., M-Qubed and Satisficing algorithm (S-alg), using the Boltzmann multiplication ensemble method. Experimental studies, in which the M-Qubed agent, the S-alg agent, and the proposed agent played ten kinds of games in self-play and in a round-robin fashion, show that the proposed algorithm can gain good payoffs in nine of them and the two internal algorithms compensate each other. Finally, we also confirmed that the learning speed of the proposed algorithm is faster than M-Qubed.

Keywords: Reinforcement learning; Game theory; Multi-agent.

1. Introduction

We humans make various decisions in daily life. In a social situation where a person's decision depends on other people's, there are complicated mutual relations such as competition and cooperation among people. Many researchers widely study game theory that models the relations among people as "games" and analyzes rational decision-making on games.

Also, we humans have an instinctive desire for survival and learn to avoid harmful, unpleasant states and approach beneficial, pleasant states by trial and error in various situations. It is due to a learning mechanism in the human brain.

In this work, we consider situations where people learn their behavior from the result of interaction with others. As a model of these situations, we discuss reinforcement learning agents that play games. Many (multi-agent) reinforcement learning algorithms have been proposed. They perform well in a certain kind of games. However, there is no one that performs well in any kind of games as we humans adapt to various, complicated situations of the real world[1]. In order to solve this problem, we construct an algorithm that performs well in any kind of games by combining two complementary reinforcement learning algorithms.

The structure of this paper is as follows. In Section 2, we shortly introduce games and reinforcement learning used in the latter sections. In Section 3, we construct a new reinforcement learning algorithm that performs well in various games by combining two state-of-the-art reinforcement learning algorithms. First, we introduce the two state-of-the-art algorithms and show some weaknesses in them. After that, we combine them to a new algorithm in which the weaknesses are compensated each other. In Section 4, we evaluate the proposed algorithm by experiments. Finally, in Section 5, we conclude this paper.

2. Background

Here we introduce game theory that models interaction among people and reinforcement learning that models the trial-and-error learning for adaptation to the environment.

2.1. *Game Theory*

Every person is always making decisions on what to do now to achieve his/her purposes. In the social environment, every decision is affected by decisions of other people. Game theory[2] analyzes the relationship among decisions mathematically.

Game theory analyzes games defined as conditions under which players interact mutually. It consists of the following four elements:

(1) Rules that govern the game,
(2) Players who decide what to do,
(3) Action strategies of the players, and
(4) Payoffs given to the players.

Game theory analyzes the confrontation and cooperation in the environment where actions of the players influence mutually. We deal with two-person simultaneous games in this work.

In a two-person simultaneous game, two players choose actions according to their strategies. After both players choose their actions, each player is given a payoff that is determined by the actions. Since the payoff of each player is determined by not only his/her action but also the associate's one, it is necessary to deliberate the associate's action to maximize payoffs.

2.2. *Reinforcement Learning*

Reinforcement learning[3] is a learning method that learns policies from interaction with the environment. An agent is defined as a decision-making entity, and the environment is everything out of the agent that interacts with the agent. The agent interacts with the environment at a discrete time step $t = 0, 1, 2, 3, \ldots$. At each time step t, the agent recognizes the current state $s^t \in S$ of the environment, where S is a set of possible states, and decides an action $a^t \in A(s^t)$ based on the current state, where $A(s^t)$ is a set of actions selectable in the state s^t. At the next step, the agent receives a reward $r^{t+1} \in \Re$ as a result of the action, and observes a new state s^{t+1}. The probability that the agent chooses a possible action a in a state s is shown as a policy $\pi^t(s, a)$. Reinforcement learning algorithms have a role to update the policy π^t at each time step and choose an action based on the policy.

3. Proposal

In this work, we consider reinforcement learning agents that interact with each other. Although there are various, complicated situations in the real world, however, there is no reinforcement learning algorithm that performs well in any kind of games. Therefore, we construct an algorithm that performs well in any kind of games by combining two complementary reinforcement learning algorithms. First, we introduce two complementary reinforcement learning algorithms and discuss the problem that they do not always perform well. After that, we propose our algorithm that combines these two algorithms.

3.1. *Two Complementary Reinforcement Learning Algorithms*

Here we introduce two complementary reinforcement learning algorithms, M-Qubed[1] and Satisficing algorithm[4], that base our algorithm.

3.1.1. *M-Qubed*

M-Qubed[1] is a state-of-the-art excellent reinforcement learning algorithm that has three strategies which can learn cooperation with the associates in various games, and avoid being exploited unilaterally. M-Qubed uses Sarsa[5] to learn the action value function $Q(s, a)$ (called Q-value) meaning the value of the action a in the state s. The state is defined as the combination of actions of the agent and its associates. $Q(s, a)$ is updated by the following rule:

$$Q^{t+1}(s^t, a^t) = Q^t(s^t, a^t) + \alpha[r^t + \gamma V^t(s^{t+1}) - Q^t(s^t, a^t)] \qquad (1)$$

$$V^t(s) = \sum_{a \in A(s)} \pi^t(s, a) Q^t(s, a) \qquad (2)$$

where s^t is the state at time t, a^t is the action at time t, $r^{t+1} \in [0, 1]$ is the payoff given by a^t in s^t, α is learning rate, γ is discount rate, and $\pi^t(s, a)$ is the probability at time t that the player takes an action a in a state s.

After M-Qubed updates the Q-value, it calculates the policy of the agent from three strategies named "Profit pursuit", "Loss aversion", and "Optimistic search". In the following, the maximin value is the secured payoff regardless of the associates given by the maximin strategy that maximizes the minimum payoff based on the payoff definition of the game.

Profit pursuit
    It takes the action with the maximum Q-value if it is larger than the discounted sum of the maximin value, or follows the maximin strategy otherwise.

Loss aversion
    It takes the action with the maximum Q-value if the accumulated loss is smaller than a threshold, or follows the maximin strategy otherwise. The accumulated loss is the difference between the accumulated payoffs and the accumulated maximin value. The threshold is determined as proportional to the number of possible states and joint actions.

Optimistic search
    The "Profit pursuit" strategy can acquire high payoffs at the moment; however it tends to produce myopic actions as a result. The "Loss aversion" strategy cannot lead cooperation with its associates, which may give high payoffs. To solve this problem, M-Qubed sets the initial Q-values to their highest possible discounted reward $1/(1 - \gamma)$, thereby learning wider strategies in perspective.

Then, the strategy is a weighted average of "Profit pursuit" and "Loss aversion", and Q-values are initialized by "Optimistic search". However, if all recently visited states have low Q-values, the strategies of the agent and its associates may be staying in a local optimum. The agent has to explore to find a solution that may give a high payoff. Hence, in this case, the strategy is changed to the weighted average of the mixed strategy described above and a completely random strategy.

3.1.2. *Satisficing algorithm*

Satisficing algorithm (S-alg)[4] is a reinforcement learning algorithm that calculates a value named the aspiration level of the agent. The agent stays in the state that gives payoffs more than its aspiration level. The algorithm is as follows.

(1) Set the initial aspiration level (α^0) randomly between the maximum payoff R_{max} and $2R_{max}$
(2) Repeat the following.

  (a) Select an action a^t

$$a^t \longleftarrow \begin{cases} a^{t-1} & \text{if } (r^{t-1} \geq \alpha^{t-1}), \\ \text{a random action otherwise.} \end{cases} \qquad (3)$$

  (b) Receive a payoff r^t and update the aspiration level

$$\alpha^{t+1} \longleftarrow \lambda \alpha^t + (1 - \lambda)r^t \qquad (4)$$

where $\lambda \in (0, 1)$ is learning rate.

S-alg is an algorithm that learns good cooperation with its associates.

3.2. *Problems of M-Qubed and Satisficing Algorithm*

Although these two algorithms are good, they also have some problems.

- M-Qubed needs long time for learning because it has multiple strategies and needs to decide which one is used. Therefore, the average payoff becomes less than S-alg in the game where only one state becomes the most suitable solution as a result of cooperation with associates.

- In the case that the associates are greedy, S-alg is exploited unilaterally because it makes the aspiration level decrease and then S-alg is satisfied with low payoffs.

- Due to insufficient search, S-alg may be satisfied with the second best payoff.

In other words, there is no algorithm that always gets high payoffs in any games. However, the problem of M-Qubed and that of S-alg are complementary. M-Qubed, which is not exploited due to the "Loss aversion" strategy and explores the environment enough, can compensate the weakness of S-alg. On the other hand, S-alg, which quickly learns cooperation, can compensate the weakness of M-Qubed. Therefore, we construct an algorithm that learns the optimal strategies in various games by combining M-Qubed and S-alg.

3.3. *Ensemble Algorithm in Reinforcement Learning*

In this research, we propose an algorithm that maximizes payoffs by combining M-Qubed and S-alg with complementary strong and weak points. As shown in Fig. 1, the algorithm holds the two reinforcement learning algorithms and makes a new strategy that combines the strategies of the two internal algorithms. Based on the action which the proposed algorithm selects, both of the internal reinforcement learning algorithms update their functions, i.e., Q-value and the aspiration level, simultaneously.

We use Boltzmann multiplication (BM)[6] as the method of combination. Based on the policy π_j^t of internal algorithm j, BM multiplies policies of both internal algorithms for each available action and determines the ensemble policy by the Boltzmann distribution. The preference values of actions are

$$p^t(s^t, a) = \prod_j \pi_j^t(s^t, a). \tag{5}$$

The resulting ensemble policy is

$$\pi^t(s^t, a) = \frac{p^t(s^t, a)^{\frac{1}{\tau}}}{\sum_{a' \in A(s^t)} p^t(s^t, a')^{\frac{1}{\tau}}} \tag{6}$$

where τ is a temperature parameter. After calculating the ensemble policy, the agent selects an action, and all internal algorithms learn from the result of this selected action.

Since S-alg gives only pure strategies, the actions except for the chosen one have zero probability. It makes M-Qubed meaningless when we use BM to combine M-Qubed and S-alg without consideration. In our method, S-alg gives a mixed strategy in which the chosen action is played with probability $p < 1$.

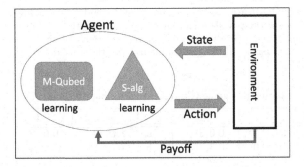

Fig. 1. Our proposed algorithm holds the two reinforcement learning algorithms and makes a new strategy. Based on the action which the proposed algorithm selects, both of the internal reinforcement algorithms update their functions simultaneously.

4. Experiments

In order to confirm the performance of the proposed algorithm, we conducted the experiment using ten two-person two-action matrix games used in the M-Qubed paper[1]. We also set the M-Qubed parameters identical to the original ones[1]. Table 1 shows the games used in the experiment.

4.1. *Experiment 1*

First, we conducted an experiment in which both players are agents having an identical algorithm, i.e., self-play. We compared M-Qubed, S-alg, and our proposed method with $p = 0.9$, 0.99, 0.999, and 0.99999. We call the agent using our proposed method $PM(p)$, where p is the probability of the action S-alg selects. The agents played one of the ten games 300 000 times, and it iterated 50 times. Table 2 shows the normalized average payoffs that were divided by the average payoff of the maximum combination(s) shown in Table 1.

In Prisoner's dilemma (PD), the average payoff of S-alg is larger than that of M-Qubed. This is because the average payoff of M-Qubed decreased due to visiting states giving small payoffs by performing many explorations to learn the cooperative action. On the other hand, M-Qubed learned the nearly optimal strategy in Security game (SG), but S-alg did not. It means that the aspiration level of S-alg decreased to the second best payoff because of the insufficient exploration. In addition, our proposed method with

Table 1. Payoff matrices of two-person two-action matrix games used in the experiment. The row player has two actions named a and b, and the column player has two actions named c and d. The values in the cells show the payoffs each player is given when the combination of actions appears (left for the row player and right for the column player). The payoffs in the bold italic face are those maximizing the sum of them.

(a) Common interest game (CIG)

	c	d
a	*1.0, 1.0*	0.0, 0.0
b	0.0, 0.0	0.5, 0.5

(b) Coordination game (CG)

	c	d
a	*1.0, 0.5*	0.0, 0.0
b	0.0, 0.0	*0.5, 1.0*

(c) Stag hunt (SH)

	c	d
a	*1.0, 1.0*	0.0, 0.75
b	0.75, 0.0	0.5, 0.5

(d) Tricky game (TG)

	c	d
a	0.0, 1.0	*1.0, 0.67*
b	0.33, 0.0	0.67, 0.33

(e) Prisoner's dilemma (PD)

	c	d
a	*0.6, 0.6*	0.0, 1.0
b	1.0, 0.0	0.2, 0.2

(f) Battle of the sexes (BS)

	c	d
a	0.0, 0.0	*0.67, 1.0*
b	*1.0, 0.67*	0.33, 0.33

(g) Chicken (Ch)

	c	d
a	*0.84, 0.84*	0.33, 1.0
b	1.0, 0.33	0.0, 0.0

(h) Security game (SG)

	c	d
a	0.84, 0.33	0.84, 0.0
b	0.0, 1.0	*1.0, 0.67*

(i) Offset game (OG)

	c	d
a	0.0, 0.0	*0.0, 1.0*
b	*1.0, 0.0*	0.0, 0.0

(j) Matching pennies (MP)

	c	d
a	*1.0, 0.0*	*0.0, 1.0*
b	*0.0, 1.0*	*1.0, 0.0*

$p = 0.99$ obtained the payoff that is higher than M-Qubed and S-alg in Offset game (OG). Since these results show that the proposed method obtained better results than (at least) one of its internal reinforcement learning algorithms, we know that it properly uses the complementary algorithms. Since the proposal with $p = 0.99$ learned the nearly optimal strategy in all games except for Offset game (OG), it is a widely usable algorithm.

Table 2. The normalized average payoffs when agents play games in self-play. The bold face means the best result among the six methods.

Game	M-Qubed	S-alg	PM(0.9)	PM(0.99)	PM(0.999)	PM(0.99999)
CIG	0.998956	0.999868	**0.999991**	0.999880	0.999884	0.999894
CG	0.974634	**0.999653**	0.565820	0.977571	0.969858	0.999457
SH	0.999241	0.999876	**0.999991**	0.999836	0.999890	0.999888
TG	0.966469	**0.999718**	0.970825	0.973407	0.972510	0.999547
PD	0.917534	**0.999774**	0.934368	0.926097	0.971011	0.999550
BS	0.984214	**0.999763**	0.986278	0.985918	0.980657	0.999641
Ch	0.988794	**0.999838**	0.989184	0.988785	0.989708	0.999562
SG	0.983062	0.700552	**0.984317**	0.984236	0.971760	0.748795
OG	0.493440	0.499923	0.019719	**0.609852**	0.491208	0.480169
MP	**1.000000**	**1.000000**	**1.000000**	**1.000000**	**1.000000**	**1.000000**

4.2. Experiment 2

Here we compared the proposed method with M-Qubed and S-alg in round-robin tournaments, in which all combinations of agents were examined. We used PM(0.99) based on the result of the Experiment 1. Again, the agents played one of the ten games 300 000 times, and it iterated 50 times. In an asymmetric game, we replaced the position of players and started the experiment again. The normalized average reward of each game is shown in Table 3. Values over 1 show that the player exploited other players and gained high payoffs.

Table 3. The normalized average payoffs when agents play games in round-robin tournaments. The bold face means the best result among the three methods.

Game	M-Qubed	S-alg	PM(0.99)
CIG	0.999266	**0.999846**	0.999734
CG	1.064534	0.833159	**1.070472**
SH	0.999394	**0.999860**	0.999688
TG	0.974606	**0.986435**	0.975419
PD	0.936898	**0.966992**	0.942708
BS	1.033065	0.901039	**1.042997**
Ch	0.988841	**0.994097**	0.988638
SG	0.935408	0.802276	**0.935854**
OG	0.565524	0.265818	**0.623308**
MP	**1.079259**	0.838132	1.077609

In Tricky game (TG), Prisoner's dilemma (PD) and Chicken (Ch), in which it is the only optimal strategy to cooperate with the associate, S-alg has gained higher payoffs than other algorithms. However, in Coordination game (CG), Battle of the sexes (BS), Security game (SG), Offset game (OG) and Matching pennies (MP), the best result is different in both players. Therefore, when the associate took a greedy strategy, S-alg was exploited because its aspiration level decreased too much and it was satisfied with small payoffs as a result. The proposed method was not exploited and it was able to learn the nearly optimal strategy in Prisoner's dilemma (PD) that M-Qubed is poor at and in Security game (SG) that S-alg is poor at.

4.3. *Experiment 3*

Here we checked whether S-alg really compensates the learning speed of M-Qubed in the proposed method with $p = 0.99$. M-Qubed, S-alg, and the proposed method played Common interest game (CIG), Stag hunt (SH), and Security game (SG) in self-play. Figure 2 shows the average payoffs, obtained from 10 iterations, of the algorithms at each time step.

Figure 2a, the result of Common interest game, shows that S-alg most quickly learned the optimal strategy by the 107th play. PM(0.99) learned the optimal strategy by around the 190th play, shortly after S-alg. M-Qubed was still learning at the 500th play. This shows that S-alg compensates the learning speed of M-Qubed in the proposed method.

Figure 2b, the result of Stag Hunt, shows that, like Fig. 2a, S-alg most quickly learned the optimal strategy by around the 150th play. Next, PM(0.99) finished learning and the average reward converged to 1 by around the 410th play. Finally, M-Qubed finished learning by around the 1500th play. This shows the same as Fig. 2a, i.e., S-alg learned the cooperation fastest and M-Qubed learned slow due to too much exploration.

However, since S-alg does not explore the environment so much, it may not learn the optimal strategy. As shown in Fig. 2c, the result of Security game (SG), S-alg finished learning first, but it did not obtain the optimal strategy because S-alg was satisfied in the second best payoff. Actually, S-alg has gained smaller payoffs compared with the other two algorithms in this game. PM(0.99) and M-Qubed obtained the nearly optimal strategy. In the proposed method, M-Qubed compensates this weakness of S-alg.

5. Conclusion

Many researchers are studying reinforcement learning algorithms to acquire strategies that maximize payoffs of individuals. However, in games that models the relation among people, there is no reinforcement learning algorithm that always performs well. In this work, we proposed an algorithm that gains large payoffs in many games by combining the complementary

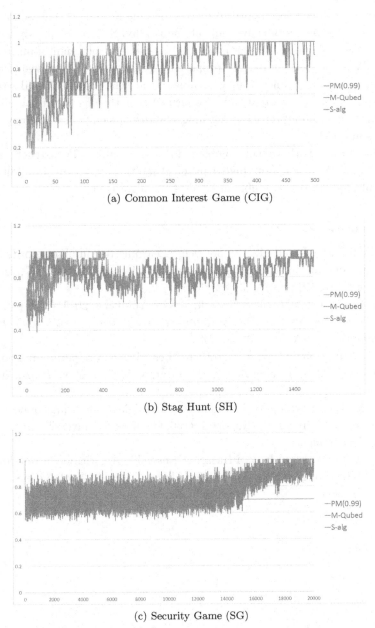

(a) Common Interest Game (CIG)

(b) Stag Hunt (SH)

(c) Security Game (SG)

Fig. 2.   Learning curves of the three algorithms in self-play in three games. Gray lines show the curve of the proposed method, blue show that of M-Qubed, and orange show that of S-alg. The x-axes show the number of games the agents play, and the y-axes show the normalized average payoffs.

reinforcement learning algorithms. We combine M-Qubed that is not exploited and explores the environment enough and S-alg that quickly learns cooperation by using the ensemble method named Boltzmann multiplication. When agents having the proposed algorithm played ten two-person two-action matrix games, they were able to learn the nearly optimal strategies of nine games. Moreover, we confirmed that the algorithm combining complementary reinforcement learning algorithms compensated for weaknesses mutually.

As a future work, we will combine more algorithms and construct a new algorithm that can acquire higher payoffs than this algorithm. In addition, we will improve the ensemble method of the algorithm.

References

1. J. W. Crandall and M. A. Goodrich, "Learning to compete, coordinate, and cooperate in repeated games using reinforcement learning", *Mach. Learn.*, vol. 82, pp. 281–314, 2011.
2. A. Okada, *Game Theory*, New ed., Tokyo: Yuhikaku, 2011. (in Japanese)
3. R. S. Sutton and A. G. Barto, *Reinforcement Learning: An Introduction*, Cambridge, MA: MIT Press, 1998.
4. J. L. Stimpson and M. A. Goodrich, "Learning To Cooperate in a Social Dilemma: A Satisficing Approach to Bargaining", in *Proc. ICML*, 2003, pp. 728–735.
5. G. A. Rummery and M. Niranjan. "On-line Q-learning using connectionist systems", Technical Report TR166, Cambridge University Engineering Department, 1994.
6. M. A. Wiering and H. van Hasselt, "Ensemble Algorithms in Reinforcement Learning", *IEEE Trans. Syst. Man. Cybern. B*, vol. 38, pp. 930–936, 2008.

FIGHTER OR EXPLORER? — CLASSIFYING PLAYER TYPES IN A JAPANESE-STYLE ROLE-PLAYING GAME FROM GAME METRICS

Kevin Fischer

Faculty of Technology, Bielefeld University, Germany
E-mail: kfischer@techfak.uni-bielefeld.de

Koichi Moriyama, Ken-ichi Fukui, and Masayuki Numao

The Institute of Scientific and Industrial Research, Osaka University, Japan
E-mail: {koichi, fukui, numao}@ai.sanken.osaka-u.ac.jp

Adaptive computer gaming aims at increasing the player's entertainment by adjusting the game's content to the player's preferences. This work explores the possibility of using gameplay statistics (called game metrics) to classify players of a short self-made Japanese-style role-playing game (JRPG) into one of two classes, namely, *Fighter* and *Explorer*. This classification is used to select the final scene of the game in order to meet the player's preferences. During this work a data collection and a subsequent experiment to evaluate the classification performance were conducted. The trained SVM classifier was able to assign the correct class to 9 out of 14 participants but showed significant weaknesses in classifying the *Fighter* class. A detailed look at these results and a discussion about the possible reasons for the discovered difficulties will be presented at the end of this work.

1. Introduction

Modern computer games feature increasingly complex interactive scenarios and a multitude of authored content. This content usually undergoes extensive playtesting in order to address the target player group's needs and preferences.

To save authoring effort and to attract a wider range of players it would be desirable if the process of game content creation and/or selection could be done automatically based on the perceived player characteristics. Existing works in this area range from difficulty adjustment to personalized content generation.

Hunicke and Chapman[1], for example, propose the Hamlet system for dynamic difficulty adjustment, which modifies the current stage of a First-Person Shooter (FPS) game, in order to keep the player in a certain predefined range of health points. A probabilistic reasoning system is employed to predict when the player is struggling and triggering adjustment measures. This includes either changing the enemies' strength or spawning health packs or ammunition off-screen if needed.

Another work by Shaker et al.[2] focuses on creating levels for the platform game Infinite Mario Bros. A single-layer perceptron is used to predict the player's fun using both controllable features of the game (number of gaps, gap width, etc.) and gameplay characteristics of the current player. This model is then used to search the space of possible stages and generate a level that maximizes the expected fun of the player.

This work deals with content adaptation of a Japanese-style role-playing game (JRPG), which is a subgenre of the computer role-playing game genre. It made its first appearance in the 1980s when the first games of this kind were released for Nintendo's Family Computer console (or Nintendo Entertainment System (NES) as it is called outside of Japan). In contrast to their western counterparts at that time, in JRPGs the player usually does not create their own party of characters but takes control over a cast of characters with own personality and motivation. Also the character advancement mechanics are severely simplified from the typical distribution of points to different ability scores. JRPGs also did the first step towards digital storytelling in a scale that was only known from books and feature films at that time.

The adaptation of this kind of story heavy game, however, poses additional challenges, since most of the content is closely tied to the game's narrative. Thus a change to the content could easily cause inconsistencies in the story logic of the game, which usually rises the need for story generation techniques.

Since narrative generation in itself is a vast field which is still not understood very well, here we choose a simple branching story approach as a first step towards content adaptation in JRPGs. In this work, gameplay characteristics of the player (game metrics) are used to distinguish two different player types, namely, *Fighters* and *Explorers*. An earlier analysis of game metrics collected by Drachen et al.[3] from a major commercial title proved that it was possible to distinguish between four distinct player types from this kind of data.

This classification is subsequently used to choose one of two alternative final scenes for the game in order to provide preferred gameplay elements for the determined player type, *i.e.*, the *Fighters* will have many opportunities for combat in their final scene whereas the *Explorers* will explore secret passageways in order to reach their goal. The final scene fitting their type will entertain the player more.

In the following sections, first a description of the game's story and structure is given. Afterwards the experimental procedure is introduced followed by the results and conclusions drawn from them.

2. Game Description

The game "The City of the Dead" is a short JRPG that was created with RPG Maker VX Ace, a game creation software by Enterbrain[a]. This tool features a map editor, a customizable database of game content like characters, enemies and items and a range of ready-to-use graphic and audio resources. Interactive game elements, so called *events*, can be defined with a very simple interface guided programming language. In addition to that, most of the game engine's source code is openly accessible in the Ruby programming language, which enables fundamental changes to the game system as well as the addition of own features to the game system.

2.1. *Gameplay*

In the game, the player moves the protagonist through several areas filled with objects and characters they can interact with. The game areas are structured in a square grid and the player can only move in discrete steps on this grid. The main interaction with the environment, *i.e.*, manipulating objects and talking to non-player characters (NPCs), is carried out by pressing a button on the gamepad.

The other major game mode is combat, which happens in a special combat scene triggered once the player encounters a hostile creature. Combat is carried out turnwise, *i.e.*, every turn the player has to choose what kind of action their own character should execute. The player has several options at their disposal: Attacking with the sword, choosing a special technique, or using an item like a healing potion. After the choice phase, the execution of the selected actions is shown and the next turn begins. This usually continues until one of the opposing sides is defeated.

---

[a]http://www.rpgmakerweb.com/products/programs/rpg-maker-vx-ace (accessed Feb. 13, 2015)

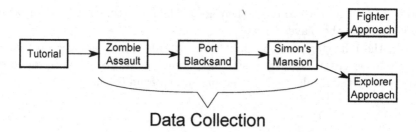

Fig. 1. Overview of the game's playable scenes

2.2. *Scene Overview*

The game's story, which was inspired by a *Fighting Fantasy* gamebook[4], revolves around Eric, a traveling mercenary, who sets out to defeat an evil undead mage terrorizing a nearby city. In total, there are 6 playable scenes (Fig. 1) which are described in the following paragraphs.

Tutorial: In the tutorial scene, Eric travels along a forest road on his search for a tavern. This short segment is used as a tutorial to introduce the player to the basic gameplay needed for the subsequent scenes.

Zombie Assault: During the night the tavern is attacked by a group of roaming undead creatures (Fig. 2a). Eric has several choices of how to defend the tavern from the zombies. He can either fight them directly, use a bottle of holy water found in another guest's room to drive them off, or move some heavy crates in front of the door to block it.

After the attack Eric learns that they have been sent by Zanbar Bone, an evil magician residing in the nearby city of Port Blacksand. After being offered a huge reward Eric sets out to stop Bone.

Port Blacksand: Port Blacksand is patrolled by Bone's undead guards. The player has to navigate Eric through the streets of the city without being seen and find a friendly wizard called Isaac to ask him for help. Isaac tells him that Zanbar Bone can only be defeated with a silver arrow and sends Eric to the house of Simon, a rich man, to acquire the silver needed for the arrow.

Simon's Mansion: Simon fearing for his life hides himself in his room and summoned a golem to protect the door. The player's task is to search

(a) Eric defending the tavern

(b) Eric fighting the golem

Fig. 2. Screenshots of the game. This game was created with RPG Maker VX Ace and these screenshots include third-party resources developed by Soichi[c], Celianna[d], and REFMAP[e], as well as those of the software manufacturer. All resource developers keep their rights

the house to find a way past the golem. Next to just fighting the golem (Fig. 2b), Eric can ask the wife to give him access to her husband or find a ritual in the mansion's library to dismiss the golem without fight. In the end, Eric receives a silver brooch which is in turn being forged into a silver arrow by a local silversmith.

[c]http://makapri.web.fc2.com/ (in Japanese, accessed Feb. 13, 2015)
[d]http://pixanna.nl/ (accessed Feb. 13, 2015)
[e]http://www.tekepon.net/fsm (in Japanese, but closed as at Feb. 13, 2015)

After acquiring the silver arrow, there are two possible ways to enter Zanbar Bone's tower.

Fighter Approach: Eric joins forces with Isaac and together they enter through the tower's front door. On the way up to the throne room, the player has to defeat several groups of enemies, all of whom need different tactics to be defeated. Finally the player has to fight Zanbar Bone himself and use the silver arrow in the right moment to kill him.

Explorer Approach: Eric is teleported to the roof of the tower to search for a secret entrance. He has to examine his surroundings to find the items and switches in order to get to the throne room. Finally the player will sneak invisibly into the room and find a good spot to shoot the silver arrow from to finish the game.

3. Experimental Procedure

To investigate whether the players of "The City of the Dead" can be classified into the two proposed types, a total of 39 players, mainly international students from Osaka University, were recruited to play the game. The first 25 participated in the data collection phase and the other 14 players took part in the actual classification experiment.

The experiment was conducted in one of the rooms of the laboratory, which was equipped with a computer using speakers and a gamepad to play the game. The participant first had to fill out a short questionnaire about demographical data like their age, gender, nationality as well as a self-assessment of their prior experience with video games in general and JRPGs in particular (on a 5-point likert scale).

Then the participant played the game. During the tutorial scene the participant could ask any questions to clarify issues about the game controls and mechanics. After that they were instructed to continue on their own for the rest of the game. The experimenter stayed in the room, out of sight of the participant, in order to offer advice in case the subject would not be able to continue on their own.

During the data collection phase, the player had to choose which of the two approaches to entering the tower of Zanbar Bone (see Section 2) they would like to take. This choice was included in a character dialogue just after arriving at the tower and the chosen scene determined the class label of the player. So if they chose to enter through the front door and fight through Bone's minions they were the *Fighter* type and otherwise the *Explorer* type.

In the classification experiment, a classifier trained with the data from the data collection phase was used to determine the player type of the participant after they had finished the three scenes prior the tower. Then, instead of the choice dialogue, one of the two final scenes was triggered automatically leading the player to the approach of the classified player type.

After finishing the game, the participant had to fill out another questionnaire with following questions about their game experience (again on a 5-point likert scale):

- How much did you enjoy the game as a whole?
- In particular, how much did you enjoy the last part of the game, after Eric entered the tower of Zanbar Bone?
- How much did you enjoy fighting against monsters in the game?
- How much did you enjoy exploring the areas of the game?

In the classification experiment an additional question was added to the post-game questionnaire, which should determine, whether the classification by the game was correct:

- If you would have had the choice how to get to Zanbar Bone's throne room, which options would you have chosen? (Enter through the front door and fight your way past all his guards / Use a secret entrance and sneak through hidden passageways)

The answer to this question was used as the actual class of the player to be compared to the classification of the system.

The characteristics of the full dataset including all 39 players can be seen in Table 1. The numbers given are the mean value along with the standard deviation in parentheses.

4. Results

Among the 25 participants of the data collection phase were 19 *Explorer* type players and 6 *Fighter* type players.

Their data were used to train a range of classifiers in order to find the most suitable for the classification task at hand. C4.5 decision trees and support vector machines (SVM) were chosen as the two main classifiers to

Table 1.   Recorded Game Metrics

Feature	Fighters	Explorers	Total Dataset
button_presses	101.83 (43.38)	96.26 (43)	97.94 (42.62)
events_triggered	34.83 (12.21)	37.48 (12.29)	36.67 (12.19)
npc_conversations	5.83 (3.93)	4.56 (3.4)	4.95 (3.57)
visited_squares	382.75 (107.97)	435.04 (93.43)	418.94 (99.72)
map_changes	25.83 (8.11)	32.41 (8.27)	30.39 (8.67)
menu_calls	8.75 (11.38)	7.04 (4.97)	7.56 (7.41)
menu_time	15s (18s)	24s (31s)	21s (28s)
battles	3.33 (3.11)	3.15 (2.66)	3.2 (2.76)
battle_turns	21.08 (18.26)	18.74 (17.27)	19.46 (17.37)
creatures_defeated	3.42 (3.32)	3.44 (2.61)	3.44 (2.8)
average_turn_time	4.4s (2.8s)	3.5s (2.3s)	3.8s (2.4s)
actions_per_battle	3.48 (1.94)	2.4 (1.41)	2.74 (1.64)
potions_used	1.75 (1.42)	1.26 (1.58)	1.41 (1.53)
deaths	0.25 (0.45)	0.11 (0.42)	0.154 (0.432)
other_gameovers	0.25 (0.62)	0.15 (0.53)	0.18 (0.56)
game_time	21m51s (4m26s)	21m40s (6m55s)	21m43s (1m39s)
VG_experience	3.08 (1.08)	2.85 (1.13)	2.92 (1.11)
JRPG_experience	2.41 (1.78)	2.48 (1.16)	2.46 (1.35)
#Subjects	11	28	39

be compared, whereas the Naïve Baysian classifier and Logistic regression were used as a baseline. The classifiers were tested against a 6-fold stratified cross-validation (to include one *Fighter* in every fold) averaged over 100 runs with different random seeds. The resulting accuracies can be seen in Table 2.

Table 2.   Accuracies of the classifiers in the data collection phase

C4.5	SVM	Naïve Bayes	Logistic Regression
0.66	0.75	0.6	0.7

The SVM classifier had the highest accuracy among the tested ones and was subsequently used in the classification experiment. Nine of the 14 participating players were classified correctly according to their answer in the post-game questionnaire (Table 3).

Table 3. Confusion matrix of the classification experiment

		Actual	
		Explorer	Fighter
Classified	Explorer	8	5
	Fighter	0	1

5. Discussion

5.1. *Underrepresentation of Fighters*

The chosen approach could classify many of the players of the second round correctly but especially the recognition of the *Fighter* class was problematic, since *Explorer* type players were overrepresented in the training set. Many of the reasons for the lack of *Fighter* examples may be rooted in flaws in game design.

Firstly, all of the battles in the game were optional and for some of them it was not obvious to the player that there was even the possibility of solving the scene by means of combat. Thus it was likely that the player's only battle throughout the game is the practice battle in the tutorial scene. The comment section of the questionnaire confirms this guess, since many participants were saying that there were too few monsters in the game.

Furthermore, the available options in the battle might have been confusing, especially since half of the participants had no or almost no experience with the JRPG genre before. The different skills of the protagonists were designed to offer interesting alternatives to just using the standard "Attack" command, but effects like confusing the enemy or having to receive some damage before stronger skills become available were most probably too complicated for total beginners. A simple rock-paper-scissors-like system of skills and enemy weaknesses would have been easier to understand and could still act as incentive to defeat the enemy faster than just with the basic attack.

As a final remark to the classification performance it should also be mentioned that the cost of a misclassification, *i.e.*, the expected dissatisfaction with the final scene, was much higher for a *Fighter* false positive than for a *Explorer* false positive. This is, again, rooted in flawed game design, since the *Fighter* final scene was considerably more challenging, especially for JRPG beginners.

5.2. Labeling Methodology

Another issue is the method of labeling the collected data points. After playing the first three scenes of the game, the protagonist meets the wizard Isaac in front of Zanbar Bone's tower. He presents the participant with two alternatives: Attacking the tower through the front door, which was intended to be an option a *Fighter* type player would choose, or entering the tower through a secret entrance, which should respectively be appealing to *Explorer* types.

The player's motivations for choosing one alternative over the other could be different from just choosing the ending that corresponds to their gameplay preference: Some players might have experienced mainly exploration during the first part of the game and now like to experience some more battles (or vice versa). Another reason (especially among adept JRPG players) for the *Explorer* approach is that many commercial JRPGs do not regularly offer a solution that does not involve combat. Thus they are inclined to choose the *Explorer* solution.

A completely different factor that should not be ignored is the way the two alternatives were presented to the player. In the given context, a single hero trying to defeat an evil mage controlling a whole city, the *Fighter* alternative perhaps sounds like a really bad idea. Some players even might have thought that this is no real option but leads directly to a game over.

In summary, it can be said that the method of determining the player type implicitly via an in-game choice, though it is unobtrusive if the player does not know what the experiment is about, has its disadvantages and may not capture the player type accurately.

5.3. Validity of Proposed Classes

A more fundamental issue is whether the proposed two classes are valid assumptions for distinguishing between actual player types. To explore the properties of the collected data, a cluster analysis using Weka's Expectation-Maximization algorithm with standard parameters was run on the full dataset (39 players, 27 *Explorers*, 12 *Fighters*). The features of the two clusters that are statistically different (one-sided Wilcox-test, $p = 0.05$) are listed in Table 4 with their mean and standard deviation.

The two clusters clearly divide the experienced JRPG players (Cluster A) from the ones that have little or no experience at all (Cluster B). The inexperienced players engage significantly more in battles and try out more options (*actions_per_battle*) than the experienced players. In general, they

Table 4. Cluster Characteristics

Attribute	Cluster A	Cluster B
battles	2.23 (1.73)	5.98 (3.13)
battle_turns	12.26 (9.76)	40.05 (17.01)
creatures_defeated	2.45 (1.96)	6.27 (2.77)
average_turn_time	3.2s (2.2s)	6.2s (2.8s)
actions_per_battle	2.33 (1.58)	3.91 (1.06)
potions_used	0.88 (1.03)	3.91 (1.06)
deaths	0 (0.43)	0.59 (0.66)
other_gameovers	0.03 (0.18)	0.59 (0.91)
game_time	19m50s (3m35s)	27m28s (5m58s)
VG_experience	3.16 (1.15)	2.25 (0.51)
JRPG_experience	2.9 (1.24)	1.2 (0.58)
Explorer	5	22
Fighter	6	6
Total	11	28

need more time to complete the first three scenes of the game and also suffer more often from a game over or death in combat. The experienced players, on the contrary, need less time to get familiar with all the game mechanics and thus concentrate on finishing the game.

Interesting is that on the one hand, most of the inexperienced players chose the *Explorer* approach, but on the other hand there is no significant difference in the typical exploration features like *button_presses*, *visited_squares*, or *map_changes* between the two clusters. This seems to support the hypothesis from the previous subsection, that the inexperienced players — though they have already completed several battles — might still be intimidated by the challenge of the *Fighter* option and thus choose the seemingly easier way of exploration. At the very least it can be said that there must be other motivations or factors that influence the decision than those captured by the chosen features.

6. Conclusion

This work introduces a set of experiments that was conducted to find out whether two different player types could be distinguished from gameplay data collected from a short JRPG. The results of these experiments reveal difficulties in reliably classifying in particular the proposed *Fighter* type.

In future works the experience acquired from conducting these experiments should be used to revise some of the addressed game design flaws. The options available in combat have to be redesigned in order to be more appealing and easier to understand for the players. The final *Fighter* scene needs some additional balancing in order to be more entertaining to less experienced participants. Finally, more battles have to be added to the game so that the players have a realistic chance to judge whether they like combat or not.

In general it has to be re-evaluated if the proposed division between *Fighters* and *Explorers* is reasonable or if it is more worthwhile to focus on another dimension of content adaption. It would also be interesting to conduct larger-scale experiments with groups consisting only of experienced or inexperienced players. In this way, it should be easier to detect genuine differences in player style than with a mixed group.

References

1. Robin Hunicke and Vernell Chapman. AI for Dynamic Difficulty Adjustment in Games. *AAAI Workshop of Challenges in Game Artificial Intelligence*, AAAI Technical Report WS-04-04, pp. 91–96, 2004.
2. Noor Shaker, Georgios N. Yannakakis, and Julian Togelius. Towards Automatic Personalized Content Generation for Platform Games. *Proc. 6th AAAI Conference on Artificial Intelligence and Interactive Digital Entertainment*, 2010.
3. Anders Drachen, Alessandro Canossa, and Georgios N. Yannakakis. Player Modeling using Self-Organization in Tomb Raider: Underworld. *Proc. IEEE Symposium on Computational Intelligence and Games*, pp. 1–8, 2009.
4. Ian Livingstone. *City of Thieves*, Puffin Books, 1983.

NODE ENERGY AND LOCATION-BASED CLUSTER HEAD SELECTION FOR THE LEACH ROUTING ALGORITHM

R. P. Damasco, M. A. Tolentino, Y. Lim and A. V. Ong[†]

Center for Networking and Information Security, De La Salle University,
Manila, Philippines
[†]*E-mail: arlyn.ong@delasalle.ph*

Wireless sensor network (WSN) is a network of small embedded systems called nodes. These nodes gather data using various sensors to monitor an event; and wirelessly pass the data to a base station for analysis. Low Energy Adaptive Clustering Hierarchy (LEACH) is a hierarchical cluster-based routing algorithm for WSNs. LEACH groups the nodes into clusters, each having a randomly selected cluster-head that acts as the gateway for its cluster-members. Since the cluster-head selection is random, the selected cluster-head may not have enough energy compared to the other nodes or might be located poorly on the network. These instances can reduce the system lifetime of the WSN. This paper introduces ClusterNet, a modification of the LEACH routing algorithm that considers the residual energy and location of the node as a metric for choosing the cluster-heads to increase the system lifetime of the WSN.

Keywords: Wireless Sensor Networks, Low Energy Adaptive Clustering Hierarchy, routing protocols

1. Introduction

A wireless sensor network (WSN) is composed of small networked devices called sensor nodes. They are commonly to monitor various events in an environment and collect data about the events to provide information to users. Wireless sensor nodes have a very wide use of application. They can be used in homes, hospitals, forestry, and traffic monitoring applications [1].

Due to potential deployment versatility, sensor nodes are commonly developed as lightweight, battery-operated devices that communicate with each other via radio transmission. These nodes have the ability for self-organization to create their own network, and are expected to operate for a long time with minimum maintenance [2].

For a sensor node to transmit data to a particular destination, it relies on a routing protocol to determine an ideal path through the network to a receiving node . Since the nodes are battery-operated devices, it is important to provide a routing protocol that can efficiently utilize the energy consumption of the nodes. One of the prominent routing protocols used for WSNs is the Low Energy Adaptive Clustering Hierarchy (LEACH) routing protocol [3], a hierarchical cluster-based routing algorithm.

LEACH uses periodic rounds to group the sensor nodes into clusters, with each cluster composed of cluster member nodes and a randomly-elected cluster-head (CH). Cluster members gather data and send these to the CH of their respective clusters; while CHs aggregate data from cluster-members and route these to a base station. Selection of CHs using LEACH may cause inefficient energy consumption within the network due to the randomness of its selection and increased node energy usage as it functions as a CH.

In identifying issues, the proponents developed ClusterNet, a routing protocol based on LEACH that takes node residual energy and physical location within the network into consideration when selecting cluster heads. The succeeding sections of this paper shall provide an overview of the mechanics and potential issues of the LEACH protocol, then discuss the modifications incorporated by ClusterNet to address these issues, and the tests performed to evaluate the effectiveness of these modifications.

2. Low Energy Adaptive Clustering Hierarchy (LEACH)

The LEACH routing algorithm utilizes periodic rounds for its operations [3]. Each round is composed of two major phases namely, the Setup Phase and Steady Phase. During the Setup Phase, the cluster-head selection and cluster set-up take place. CHs are elected randomly using a priori that determines the desired amount of CHs in the network. Specifically, each node n generates a random number between 1 and 0. This number is then compared to the threshold $T(n)$. Equation (1) is used by LEACH to compute for the threshold used by LEACH to control cluster head numbers.

$$T(n) = \begin{cases} \dfrac{p}{1 - p*(r \, mod(\frac{1}{p}))}, & if \, n \in G \\ 0, & Otherwise \end{cases} \tag{1}$$

In this equation, p refers to the percentage of nodes desired to become cluster heads; r is the current round; and G is the set of nodes that have not been cluster heads in the last $1/p$ rounds. If the generated random value is less than the threshold $T(n)$ then it becomes a CH, else it becomes the non-CH node. Once the CHs are elected, each of them uses the Carrier Sense Multiple Access (CSMA) MAC layer protocol to broadcast an advertisement message to other nodes in the network. The non-CH nodes that receive the advertisement message then decide the cluster they will be joining based on the signal strength from the CHs that send the message to them. The non-CH nodes reply to the CH they have chosen to join a particular cluster.

Following this cluster organizing phase is the Steady Phase where the transmit schedule is created and data transmission take place. In this phase, the CHs create a Time Division Multiple Access (TDMA) schedule for their own cluster-members and assign it to the members via multicast so that member nodes are allocated a data transmission slot. Then, non-CH nodes send their sensed data to their CH only during their assigned schedule. The CHs compress all the data received from their cluster-members and relay these to the network base station. When the current round ends, the whole process repeats [3].

Compared to cluster members that transmit only during assigned schedules, nodes assigned to be CH expend more energy due to the need for transmitters to stay active for the entire round to receive data from members and aggregate these for sending to the base station. In this regard, the random selection of CHs in the LEACH protocol presents three possible issues. First, when using such a selection method, the CHs selected for a round may have low energy – presenting the risk of a CH exhausting its remaining energy before a round ends. Second, the number of nodes elected to be CH also relies on a factor of randomness. This may cause the network to have too many nodes functioning as CHs [4]. Third, CHs elected may not be ideally located within the network, resulting in large differences in cluster sizes. Some CHs may have to service a large number of cluster members, while others may have only a few. All of these factors contribute to ineffective distribution of the energy consumption of nodes in the network, leading to a reduction of overall network lifetime.

3. ClusterNet

To address the issues identified, the proposed routing algorithm, ClusterNet, modifies the cluster setup phase of the LEACH algorithm. It introduces the calculation for a reasonable number of cluster heads to elect given the network size, and elects CHs by considering both residual node energy and node location as selection criteria.

3.1. *First Round Operations*

The ClusterNet algorithm closely follows the original LEACH algorithm for the first round of transmissions. It assumes that all the nodes at the start of the round have their power sources at full capacity. During cluster head selection and cluster setup, Each node computes for the threshold *t* using Eq. 1 then uses a random number for comparison with this threshold to determine whether it shall function as a CH or a non-CH.

During the steady phase when data transmission takes place, ClusterNet nodes piggyback Received Signal Strength (RSS) information from its neighbor nodes to the base station. The base station to uses this RSS information to construct a matrix containing the distance of the nodes to each node on the network. The base station then uses multidimensional scaling (MDS) on the distance matrix to calculate the approximate x and y location of the nodes in the network. This in effect provides the base station with a map of the network

3.2. *Succeeding Round Operations*

Starting from the second round onwards, each node must send its residual energy information to the base station at the beginning of the cluster setup phase. Using the residual energy information sent by the nodes, the base station determines the number of nodes still active in the network and computes for the reasonable number of CHs given the current network size using Eq. (2), where *numNodes* is the number of nodes alive in the current round. The resulting value sets the number of nodes to become CH for the current round.

$$R\left(numNodes\right) = \frac{\sqrt{numNodes}}{2} \tag{2}$$

The base station then simulates the cluster-head selection step by first selecting $R\left(numNodes\right)$ of tentative CHs on its network map using random selection. This is followed by the rest of the cluster setup phase to evaluate the effectiveness of the resulting cluster membership if the tentative setup is followed.

For each resulting cluster, the base station calculates for the cluster centroid by taking the average x and y positions of all members of the cluster. The final selection of CH for a cluster is then determined using the residual energy reported by each node; and the distances of each node from the calculated cluster centroid. For each node i in the cluster, a CH desirability score S is computed as:

$$S = ((netLen - dist(node_i, centroid) * 0.5) \\ + (battery(node_i) * 0.5)) \tag{3}$$

Where *netLen* is a value representing network dimensions, *dist(node_i, centroid_j)* is the distance of the current node to the current centroid; and *battery(node_i)* represents the is the residual energy of the current node. The node with the highest resulting score S among nodes of a cluster is then selected as the CH of the cluster.

The desirability score is computed as such in order to place equal weight on the proximity of a node to the cluster centroid, and its remaining energy stores as factors for CH suitability. Nodes that have the most residual energy and are as close as possible to cluster centroids are likely to be selected by the base station to become CHs. In case of clusters that have only a CH and no other members, the tentative CH is demoted to a non-CH node.

The base station broadcasts the IDs of the selected cluster heads for the current round to the network to notify these nodes. The rest of the round proceeds to the steady phase. This process repeated for the succeeding rounds with the residual energy information of nodes to be transmitted to the base station at the beginning of each round.

4. Performance Evaluation

The performance of ClusterNet is compared against the LEACH algorithm through simulation. For each simulation, the nodes are deployed in random locations in the simulation space with the following parameters in Table 1.

The simulation scenario assumes that nodes are non-mobile and that the base station has a renewable power source.

Table 1. ClusterNet and LEACH test simulation parameters

Parameter	Value
Network size	500 x 500
Node count	115
Location of base station	250, 250
Priori	0.45
Round length	30s

72

Parameter	Value
Node battery capacity	750 mAh
Idle cost	40.5 mAh
Sleep cost	0.045 mAh
Transmit Cost	74.25 mAh
Receive Cost	40.5 mAh
Processing Cost	229.5 mAh

4.1. Node Residual Energy Evaluation

The average residual energy of nodes for each algorithm is measured at every round to determine whether the use of location and residual energy for selecting cluster heads results in a more gradual loss of energy for the nodes in the network. The results of these tests are illustrated in Fig. 1.

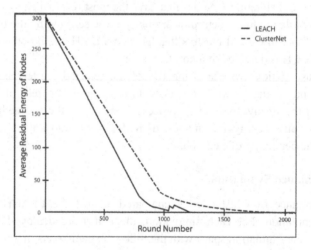

Fig. 1. Average node residual energy per round

It can be observed from the results that the average residual energy of nodes using the LEACH algorithm rapidly decreases over time. This is because the random selection of cluster heads may cause an irregular number of members in every cluster. Some clusters may have few members; while others may have disproportionately more members as the other clusters causing their CHs to utilize more energy in the same round for processing traffic from members. ClusterNet factors in node location in order to center CHs as much as possible within a cluster. This results in a more equal distribution of nodes among neighboring clusters.

Additionally, the LEACH method for selecting CHs may also cause single-node clusters to be formed with the lone node defaulting to cluster head functions. In such cases, the CH needlessly expends energy keeping its receiver active to listen to non-existent members. ClusterNet, on the other hand performs initial CH planning so that any tentative CHs that will have no member nodes can be demoted to function as a non-CH and join another cluster. This saves energy for the demoted node as it would then need to keep its transceiver active only when it is scheduled to transmit within its new cluster.

The effect of these adjustments - redistribution of nodes per cluster and reassignment of lone CHs as member nodes of another clusters - performed by ClusterNet to the network topology is illustrated in Fig. 2. The before image shows the existence of clusters with a single cluster head with no members. After adjustment, these cluster heads have been demoted into members of nearby clusters.

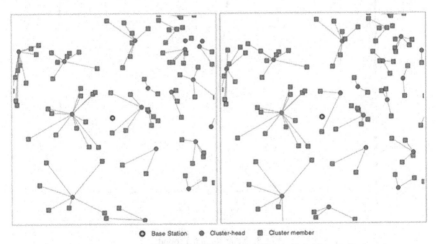

○ Base Station   ● Cluster-head   ■ Cluster member

Fig. 2. Cluster membership before (left) and after (right) cluster head adjustment

4.2. Network Lifetime Evaluation

To evaluate the system lifetime of ClusterNet and LEACH, each of these algorithms is simulated until all network nodes have exhausted their energy stores. The round at which the first node death and exhaustion for all nodes occurs is observed. Table 2 shows results of these tests.

Table 2. ClusterNet and LEACH network lifetime Comparison

Algorithm	First Node Death	Network Lifetime
LEACH	703 rounds	1140 rounds
ClusterNet	811 rounds	2401 rounds

Based on the results, ClusterNet offers a small improvement in terms of time before the first node death occurs. It can be observed however, that the overall network lifetime is more than double that of LEACH. From Fig. 3, which illustrates the node count as the simulation progresses per algorithm, it can also be observed that node failure in the network occurs more gradually in ClusterNet when compared to LEACH.

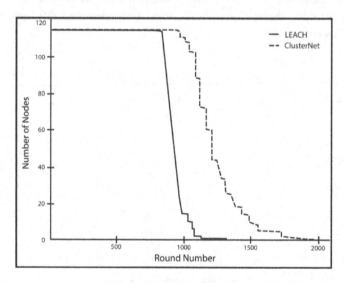

Fig. 3. Node count per round

The cause of the longer lifetime of nodes in ClusterNet may be attributed to the consideration of residual energy when selecting CHs. As a CH node proceeds through a round, it expends relatively more energy compared to non-CH nodes in its cluster. This node begins the following round with a lower amount of residual energy compared to its neighboring nodes which previously functioned as its members. When this lower residual energy is reported to the base station, it then becomes less likely for this node to be selected again as a

CH for the succeeding round, allowing it to conserve energy as it begins the next round as a non-CH. Because of this, nodes in the network take turns becoming a CH; and nodes last longer on the average compared to those in a LEACH network where random selection may cause nodes to function as CH for several consecutive rounds.

5. Conclusion

ClusterNet has made a significant difference to the original LEACH routing algorithm by modifying how and where the cluster-head selection is done. By moving the computation for the cluster-head selection from the nodes to the base station, energy consumption needed for calculation was reduced from the nodes. Since the base station is assumed to have unlimited energy compared to the nodes, transferring cluster-head selection to the base station reduces energy expenditure at the nodes.

ClusterNet computes for the reasonable number of cluster-heads on the network based on the number of currently alive nodes. The algorithm then selects cluster heads by accounting for the residual energy of a node as well as its location in a network.

These methods serve to further improve energy efficiency resulting to network lifetimes that double that of the original LEACH routing algorithm. In addition, the techniques used results to alternation of the role of CH and more even distribution of energy consumption among nodes in the network. As such, nodes stay alive longer on the average, allowing the network to maintain a wide over all coverage of the monitored environment for a longer period of time.

References

1. L. Garcia Villalba, A. Sandoval Orozco, A. Cabrera and C. Barenco Abbas, Routing Protocols in Wireless Sensor Networks, in *a special issue of Sensors*. **9**, 11 (2009).
2. M. Perillo and W. Heinzelman, *Wireless Sensor Network Protocols. In Fundamental Algorithms and Protocols for Wireless and Mobile Networks*, (2005). http://www.ece.rochester.edu/courses/ECE586/readings/perillo.pdf.
3. M. Handy, M. Haase and D. Timmerman, Low energy adaptive clustering hierarchy with deterministic cluster-head selection, in *4th IEEE Conference on Mobile and Wireless Communications Networks*, (2002).

4. W. Heinzelman, A. Chandrakasan and H. Balakrishnan, An application-specific protocol architecture for wireless microsensor networks. In *IEEE Transactions on Wireless Communications*. **1**, 4 (2002).
5. Magsino, K., Srikanth Kamath, H. 2009. Simulations of Routing Protocols of Wireless Sensor Networks, in *World Academy of Science, Engineering and Technology*, (2009).
6. S. K. Singh, M. P. Singh, and D. K. Singh, Routing Protocols in Wireless Sensor Networks: A Survey, in *International Journal of Computer Science & Engineering Society (IJCSES)*, **1**, 2 (2010).

GENRE CLASSIFICATION OF OPM SONGS THROUGH THE USE OF MUSICAL FEATURES*

J. A. Deja[†], K. Blanquera, C. E. Carabeo and J. R. Copiaco

*College of Computer Studies, De La Salle University,
Manila, Philippines*
[†]E-mail: jordan.deja@dlsu.edu.ph
www.dlsu.edu.ph

A dataset is built into a model for the classification of OPM songs into ten specific genres. Low-level musical features in the form of digital signals, like Spectral Centroid, Mel-Frequency Cepstral Coefficients among others, were collected to build the data set. A collection of 1000 songs, having 100 in-stances as representatives for each of the 10 genres from songs sang and com-posed by Filipino artists were used as data for the features in building the model. Different classifiers where employed to test and see which musical features specific for Filipino music are highlighted and can be attributed for further study. A multi-layer perceptron was selected most optimal for the model building. Additional features, genres have yet to be incorporated into the study in order to produce a set of more well-refined results.

Keywords: multilayer perceptron, music features, music classification, genre, OPM.

1. Introduction

The task of classifying music into its respective genre with the use of their respective features have been done before on a wide array of types and sources of music. However, more studies have yet to be done on the analysis of musical features specific for Original Pinoy Music (OPM). Generally, music of the Philippines which is referred to as OPM includes performances, and compositions in various genre and styles done by Filipinos. The study revolves around enabling machines who understand signals and numbers to be able to classify specifically OPM into a certain genre, data of which are of auditory nature. With the right conversion process, music of such format can be losslessly transformed into a readable format such as a .wav file. A machine learning task

---

* This work is supported by etc, etc.
[†] Work partially supported by grant 2-4570.5 of the Swiss National Science Foundation.

is employed in building and validating the model. The specific methodologies and algorithms employed will be discussed in the next sections of this paper highlighting the key features that make Filipino music unique along with the key results. Future work are also discussed in the latter parts of the paper which includes involving annotations and a natural language processing task.

2. Review of Related Literature

The study employs existing methodologies involving the same task of classification and prediction. A wide array of possible solutions, especially on the use of machine learning algorithms can be chosen from and as such, they have to be carefully-selected to which would yield the best results. The succeeding paragraphs discuss these accuracies separately.

High levels of classification accuracy have been achieved using machine learning techniques. One study [6] in particular yielded accuracies of 90% or higher. Fujinaga and McKay used kNN and neural networks. They placed great value on high-level features. Additionally, using a larger set of 'meaningful features' provides better results. Another study [8] focused on rhythm and pitch. They used a Gaussian Classifier as well as kNN on 10-fold Cross Validation. In [12], the study provides an in-depth review into musical features and the recognition of instruments. Moreover, the instruments within the study was also linked to respective genres. For each instrument in the study, Fuhrmann assessed the musical features and its implications on the sound produced. The link is also made between similar-sounding instruments and the genres they belong to. Similarly, Fuhrmann used Weka to run classifiers and investigated Spectral features and MFCC, among others, in the study.

Xu et. al [9], used the Support Vector Machine to classify a set of 60 songs. They used a 'multi-layer' approach wherein songs are initially sorted into pop/classical and rock/jazz before they are put through a second Support Vector Machine, or another 'layer', which would sort the songs between the two genres of the parent node. For example, the second layer will classify songs between pop and classical if it was sorted into pop/classical in the first SVM layer. The researchers also tested their data set using other classifiers to assess the quality of their multi-layered SVM approach. Compared to the Hidden Markov Model, kNN and Gaussian mixture model, the multi-layered SVM approach had the least amount of error at 6.86%.

Neumayer and Rauber [14] combined text and low-level audio features for genre classification. The study involves trials of classification using audio only, text only and a combination of both. The musical features used include fluctuation patterns (rhythm pattern), rhythm histograms and Statistical Spectrum Descriptors. Out of all trials conducted, the best classification accuracy is the result of a combination of lyrics, or text, and rhythm patterns.

A tempo-centric study proved the importance of tempo is important in accurate genre classification [15]. Based on their findings, using tempo, alone, was able to reach 80% classification accuracy which supports their claim. However, they used only one out of many features that contribute to rhythm. One cannot automatically assume that accuracy of classification will improve if more descriptors are added.

3. Methodology

The study included the following phases namely: (1) Dataset building, (2) Feature Selection, and the (3) Model-building and classification task as based from similar works like [4-5] and [8]. The specifics are discussed in the following subsections:

3.1. Data Set Building

The data set of 1,000 songs was created by first obtaining a list of songs per genre. Songs must fit the criteria of an OPM classification wherein it must be originally composed by a Filipino. Similarly, songs with purely-English lyrics, purely-Filipino lyrics and a mix of both languages were accepted. The 1,000 songs were divided into 10 genres where each genre is represented by 100 instances. The labeled genre where each song falls under was determined using online retailers who have made pre-classifications, such as iTunes and kabayancentral.com, a web site that caters to Filipino music. Table I shows the list of genres used for this study as based from [11]:

Table I. List of Genres and their description

Genre	Short Description
Gospel	common praise songs
Rock	popular songs with loud drum combinations
Soft Rock	similar to rock but of higher frequency for drums
Acoustic	voice and guitar, no-drum accompaniment
Rap	with poetic words pronounced in slightly-fast tempo
Children	songs meant for children
Christmas	commonly played during the holiday seasons
Jazz	songs of lower frequency, with high tempos
Reggae	songs with a saxophone accompaniment generally
Special	a special category for the popular songs that became hits

The music files were all converted to the same format: .wav. This was done because jAudio, the feature extracting program, primarily accepts this type of file. The program can accept .mp3 files as well but due to various types of encoding, converting to .wav ensured more uniformity. After conversion, the songs, as a whole, were loaded to jAudio which extracted both high and low-level music features. Refer to Appendix A. for the complete list of these features.

3.2. *Feature Selection and Extraction*

Each of the instances in the data set represented one of the ten genres where their musical features have been extracted with the use of jAudio. Since the number of musical features were too many for the machine learning task, feature selection has to be performed in order to trim down the list of features into only the significant and relevant ones. A total of 73 features were extracted and acquired per instance (See Appendix A for a full list of extracted musical features). The list of these 73 features were generated by a series of feature selection tasks done with the help of WEKA.

Prior to the selection of these 73 features, several attribute-evaluator modules were ran in order to get the best features fit for the model such as Wrapper, CfsSubsetEval among many others. Several seaarch techniques such as the Ranker and Exhaustive search were employed to further refine the selection. From almost 600 musical features, the feature selection task ended up with 73 features, which were ranked based on their information gain and content. From these 73 features, 6 top musical features were most commonly-picked by the different attribute evaluators with WEKA. To further understand the contents of the results, the authors have taken the liberty of highlighting these 6 features and their respective short descriptions based from existing studies as well:

- The Spectral Centroid feature relates to how brightly textures and high frequencies are of music.
- The Spectral Roll Off represents the '95th percentile of the power spectral distribution' [7]. When applied, it helps differentiate voiced and unvoiced sounds. Higher levels refer to unvoiced speech which also contains higher energy while lower levels refer to voiced speech.
- Spectral Flux measures the change of the spectral shape. How quickly the spectral shape changes is different for music and speech. This includes the

spectral change when words are spoken like when the speaker transitions between vowels and consonants [7]

• Mel-Frequency Cepstral Coefficients or MFCC is a low-level feature which pertains to the short-term strength of a particular sound. This can be used to model 'subjective pitch and frequency content of audio sounds' [11].

• Linear Predictive Coding or LPC is used to analyze speech as it represents the spectral envelope. The spectral envelope helps determine timbre.

• The Zero Crossings rate is the rate at which signals change between positive and negative. High values of this are indicative of noisy sounds [5].

3.3. *Model-building and Classification*

The dataset was divided into its training data and test data. The training data were subjected to several machine learning algorithms in order to determine which produced the accuracy fit for the entire data set. They were tested with k-NN, j48, Naïve-Bayes, Linear regression, Multi-layer perceptron and Support vector machine classifiers.

For k-NN, the data set was ran for several values of k, ranging from 1 to 30. Similarly, the data set was tested for several values of h (hidden layers) ranging from 1 to 75 for multi-layer perceptron and values of c (cost function) ranging from 1 to 1,000,000, for support vector machines.

After the series of training, multi-layer perceptron was chosen to build the final model for genre classification. The model was built with the use of the test data following a 10-fold cross validation approach. From the results of the testing, the final analysis and relationships specific to OPM and its classification, were discovered. These will be discussed in the succeeding section of this paper.

4. Results and Discussion

The k-Nearest Neighbor classifier is a form of lazy algorithm [1]. It checks an instance's k number of nearest neighbor using the Euclidean distance between them. The instance's closeness to neighboring instances determines which class the instance belongs to [2]. For this classifier, the accuracy of the results depended on the value of k. This classifier produced above average results. J48 is an open source Java implementation of the C4.5 algorithm in the Weka data mining tool. With feature selection alone, this classifier was able to provide excellent results. Naïve-Bayes classifier is a probabilistic classifier based on the so-called Bayesian or Bayes' theorem [3]. It's suited for inputs with high dimensionality. Bayes' theorem is important to the mathematical manipulation of conditional probabilities. The results is derived from the more basic axioms of probability. The authors have discovered that the dataset is not built to be classified by Naïve-Bayes after the series of experiments. It gave inadequate results in classifying. Moreover, feature selection had little changes to the percentage of correctly classified instances and the Kappa statistic of the dataset. Support Vector Machines (SVM) makes use of N-dimensional hyperplanes [10]. The hyperplanes optimally separates the data into two categories. They are related to neural networks which makes it a "close cousin" of multilayer perceptrons. The group tested cost functions over 500,000. From 700,000 to 1 million cost function just to see how it worked, it improved little by little in which it only improved in a logarithmic manner which is deemed to be not very significant. Though, as the cost function increases, so does the kappa statistic. And the kappa statistic is almost near the value of 1, which indicates that the data set may be too overfitted for the test.

Multilayer perceptron (MLP) is a feedforward neural network with one or more layers between the input and output layer [16] Feedforward means that data flows in one direction from input to output layer (forward) through interconnected neurons [16]. This type of network is trained with the backpropagation learning algorithm. The Multilayer Perceptron yielded some of the best results out of all trials. The learning rate was consistently kept at 0.3. The low value of the learning rate gives the machine more tries to fine tune the classification in addition the number of hidden layers gave the machine enough filters of the features to fine tune its classification on the data set. The Multilayer Perceptron works well with data that is not linearly separable much like the data set used. Additionally, aside from doing a classification for each of the 10 genres all in all, series of 1 vs All experiments for each genre were performed using multi-layer perceptron to be able to derive conclusions specific for each genre.

Table II. Model Building Results

Classifier	# of h layers	Accuracy	Kappa Statistic	MSE	RMSE
Multi-layer perceptron	73	83.5%	0.8167	0.043	0.1651

Two testing modes were done namely 10-fold cross validation and Test set method. The data set was tested with increasing values of *h* for the hidden layers, and as seen in Fig. I, there is a growth and sudden decline in the rate of accuracy when a certain number of *h* hidden layers are prescribed.

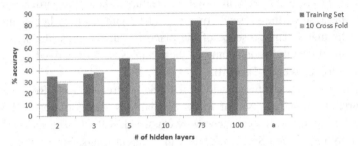

Fig. 1 Percent accuracy of each MLP trial with different *h*-values

The value for *a* is a predefined number in Weka which equates to the following

$$a = \frac{N_c + N_f}{2} \tag{1}$$

Where N_c represents the total number of classes or labels for the data set and N_f represents the total number of features excluding the labels.

Table III. Confusion Matrix for MLP with 73 hidden layers

a	b	c	d	e	f	g	h	i	j	Classified as
92	0	1	0	1	0	0	3	2	1	a = Gospel
1	**86**	9	1	0	0	1	1	1	0	b = Rock
2	2	**87**	2	1	2	1	1	1	1	c = Soft Rock
0	1	9	**80**	0	0	4	3	2	1	d = Acoustic
0	0	7	9	**86**	1	1	1	2	2	e = Special
0	0	0	1	1	**91**	1	4	0	2	f = Rap
1	0	3	0	0	0	**91**	4	0	1	g = Children
4	1	4	2	0	2	2	**82**	2	1	h = Christmas
2	0	4	4	1	1	2	3	**80**	3	i = Jazz
1	1	3	0	1	0	2	2	1	**89**	j = Reggae

Rock, Soft Rock and Acoustic are often confused for each other. They are not distinct to begin with as they are more often confused for other genres compared to the rest of the genres in the data set. Rock was more incorrectly classified into Soft Rock than other genres. Additionally, both Soft Rock and, especially Acoustic, are often confused as other genres. Rock, Soft Rock and Acoustic are consistently incorrectly classified into the other genres. This indicates that these three genres must bear a similarity to each other as well as other genres in terms of musical low-level features. Acoustic garners errors potentially because of the presence of the acoustic guitar which bears similar signals to the piano. The presence of the piano in other genres like Jazz, for example, can cause confusion. Some of these analyses were derived from the confusion matrix as seen in Table III.

Rock is primarily confused with Soft Rock, wherein 6% of Rock songs were incorrectly classified as Soft Rock. Special was also confused as Rock, wherein 5% Special songs were incorrectly classified as Rock. The same artists appears in both Rock and Soft Rock but with different songs. For example, the band *Sponge Cola* appears in Rock and then in Soft Rock also. Some songs, although they appeared in differing genres, came from the same album. This and the similarity in artist may be the reasons for the confusion. In addition, Special was also most incorrectly classified into Rock and Soft Rock. This shows how Rock and Soft Rock even confuse the same genres. The similarity between the genres may also be due to how Soft Rock is a 'child' or subgenre of Rock.

Christmas is also less distinct compared to other genres. It is most confused with Rock, Soft Rock, Acoustic and Jazz. If to be reclassified, the songs based on sound instead of content, some would fall under the Rock, Soft Rock, Acoustic and Jazz. Some artists under this genre are prominent in Rock, for example. Their original Christmas songs or versions of it were included in the data set. This is may be the source of the error in classification. The songs in the Christmas genre have been classified as such based on its topic, not the sound or style. What makes a song be categorized as Christmas is perhaps not so much it's sound or melody but its content. Because of this, a multi-modal (audio and text) approach is more appropriate like what Neumayer and Rauber used in [14].

The Special category tends to confuse most classifiers since the it is based on the current trend of popular songs. These songs, if reclassified, may belong to a different genre. For example, the song *"Ako'y Sayo at Ika'y akin lamang"* revived by Daniel Padilla is a popular song but the it could also be classified under Acoustic. The Special genre was intended to encompass songs that are popular or mainstream. This means that songs may be better suited for other genres if popularity is not an aspect.

Table IV. Linear Regression results for Children Genre

Genre	Correlation Coefficient	MAE	RMSE	RAE	RRSE
Children	0.7423	0.1234	0.201	68.5493%	67.0116%

Using the Linear Regression classifier with the training set methods, Children got the highest correlation coefficient as seen from Table IV. Of all the genres, the features of Children are the most closely-associated with each other. Because of this, Children is one of the more correctly classified and distinguishable among the genres. Rap and Gospel also had good results. Comparing all the genres, the lowest number of correlation coefficient is the Special genre which consists of popular music, which was pre-classified primarily because of the songs' popularity.

Based on results from the Linear Regression trials, an understanding of the features that comprise and distinguish a genre can be gained. First, the attributes that make Acoustic are of high frequency and of low irregular beats. The low value of Spectral Centroid which means that it has low frequency akin to bass or guitar makes sense because acoustic songs are usually comprised primarily of guitars chords. The Spectral Rolloff is also relatively high which indicates beats that are closer together whereas electric guitars also have this property [13] The low Compactness value means that beats are irregular or inconsistent. Second, the Children genre is characterized by irregular, weak beats and are less noisy. The high Spectral Centroid values mean that these songs are brighter in tone. Third, Christmas songs are less noisy overall, tend to have stronger beats and these beats are farther apart from each other. Fourth, Gospel songs are not noisy and have low beats that are closer together. The high value of Spectral Rolloff denotes the closeness of the beats and high frequencies. High Rolloff values are also associated with the Hammond organ [13]. The low value of Spectral Centroid denotes the lowness of the beats. Fifth, Jazz features beats are closer together, indicated by high Spectral Rolloff values. The high Rolloff and MFCC values also indicate high frequencies which is characteristic in the saxophone and piano as well as the trumpet [13]. The beats are also strong or loud in sound, indicated by the high Strength of Strongest Beat. Sixth, Special songs have louder, stronger beats that are closer together and features wise are not uniformed since they have been based mostly on their popularity levels. Seventh, Rap has low beats that are farther apart but are very powerful as indicated by the high value of Root Mean Square Overall Standard Deviation. Eighth, Reggae has lower, more powerful beats that are farther apart akin to a

86

tuba or bass. The high values of Area of Method of Moments of MFCC's indicate higher frequency fluctuations which is characteristic of the saxophone [6]. Ninth, Rock has strong, powerful beats, indicated by the Strength of Strongest Beat, that are low and close together. The high Rolloff values present in Rock songs are also possessed by the electric guitar [6]. Lastly, Soft Rock has weaker beats and are less noisy over-all.

5. Conclusion and Future Work

Musical features, especially low-level features are useful in the classification of genres of OPM songs. They are good indicators of pitch, brightness, loudness, frequency, timbre and musical instruments involved. Although the accuracy of classification vary according to the classifier, the data set is more suited to MLP. Naive-Bayes, kNN and J48 all yielded results with low accuracy. Spectral Centroid, Rolloff, Zero Crossings and MFCC are among the most indicative musical features. These can even help determine the instruments involved. Children songs, followed by Rap and Gospel are the most distinct. Related genres are more difficult to differentiate because of shared style, instruments or voice. For example, Rock is related to Soft Rock. Special, or popular music, and Christmas songs are challenging to define based on audio only. They can be reclassified into different genres if popularity and context are not factors. Errors and noise are likely caused by inclusion of the same artists and songs from the same album in more than one genre.

The data set was built mostly on the .wav files of 1000 different songs, where the repetition of common artists are found in several genres (for example: Bamboo is seen in Rock, Hard Rock and Acoustic, etc). The data set can be refined if it would be ensured that all instances are unique up to the artist level, or simply, avoid the appearance of artists/performers in multiple genres. The songs used for the data gathering were rendered audio from studio and as such, the data cannot be atomized down to the layer-level (such as one layer for voice, for acoustics, for percussion, rhythm, etc) because of legal and copyright constraints. Should these be acquired, an in-depth further analysis of even the low level features can be reviewed for classification.

To further improve the goals of the study, a natural language processing task along with annotations can be performed to have a classification of these OPM songs by genre down to the lyrics level: a process where aside from the musical features, these attributes can be cross-analyzed with actual lyrics for the instance at time t in a song. This way, annotating the lyrics with a corresponding emotion can provide further insights and relationship between the genre implied by a certain song. Hypothetically speaking, a song maybe according to its musical features, rock-like but because of its lyrics may differ and be classified into something different like Children or Christmas songs.

Additional genres of Filipino music should also be added like the lesser-popular but more cultural forms such as Kundiman, Folk and Tribal (Badjao, Aeta, Tivoli, etc.) genres which are unique for Filipinos and can be categorized as OPM as well. Lastly, a prototype can be implemented, to verify the features and relationships established with the existing model, or lead to the design of a music archive similar to what Azcarraga and Manalili did in [17].

References

1. Cunningham, Padraig and Delany, Sarah Jane. (2007). "k-Nearest Neighbour Classifiers."
2. Muja, Mauris and Lowe, David. (2009)."Fast Approximate Nearest Neighbours With Automatic Algorithm Configuration". University of British Columbia.
3. Zhang, Harry. (2004). "The Optimality of Naive Bayes". FLAIRS2004 conference.
4. Basili, R., Serafini, A., & Stellato, A. (2004, October). "Classification of musical genre: a machine learning approach." In ISMIR.
5. McKay, Cory, and Ichiro Fujinaga. "Automatic Genre Classification Using Large High-Level Musical Feature Sets." ISMIR. 2004.
6. Peeters, Geoffroy. (2004). "{A large set of audio features for sound description (similarity and classification) in the CUIDADO project}."
7. Scheirer, Eric, and Malcolm Slaney. (1997). "Construction and evaluation of a robust multifeature speech/music discriminator." Acoustics, Speech, and Signal Processing, 1997. ICASSP-97., 1997 IEEE International Conference on. Vol. 2. IEEE, 1997.
8. Tzanetakis, George, and Perry Cook. (2002). "Musical genre classification of audio signals." Speech and Audio Processing, IEEE transactions on 10.5: 293-302.
9. Xu, Min, et al. "HMM-based audio keyword generation." Advances in Multimedia Information Processing-PCM 2004. Springer Berlin Heidelberg, 2005. 566-574.
10. Artificial Intelligence - foundations of computational agents -- 7.3.2 Linear Regression and Classification. (n.d.). Retrieved March 3, 2014, from http://artint.info/html/ArtInt_179.html
11. Pachet, F., & Cazaly, D. (2000). A taxonomy of musical genres. In *RIAO*(pp. 1238-1245).

12. Fuhrmann, F. (2012). *Automatic musical instrument recognition from polyphonic music audio signals* (Doctoral dissertation, PhD thesis, Universitat Pompeu Fabra).
13. Xu, C., Maddage, M. C., Shao, X., Cao, F., & Tian, Q. (2003, April). Musical genre classification using support vector machines. In *Acoustics, Speech, and Signal Processing, 2003. Proceedings. (ICASSP'03). 2003 IEEE International Conference on* (Vol. 5, pp. V-429). IEEE.
14. Neumayer, R., & Rauber, A. (2007). Integration of text and audio features for genre classification in music information retrieval. In *Advances in Information Retrieval* (pp. 724-727). Springer Berlin Heidelberg.
15. Gouyon, F., Dixon, S., Pampalk, E., & Widmer, G. (2004, June). Evaluating rhythmic descriptors for musical genre classification. In *Proceedings of the AES 25th International Conference* (pp. 196-204).
16. Gardner, M. W., & Dorling, S. R. (1998). Artificial neural networks (the multilayer perceptron)--a review of applications in the atmospheric sciences. *Atmospheric environment, 32*(14-15), 2627-2636.
17. Azcarraga, A. & Manalili, S. (2011). Design of a Structured 3D SOM as a Music Archive. In *Advances in Self-Organizing Maps* (pp. 188-197). Springer-Berlin Heidelberg.

DYNAMIC AND INDIVIDUAL EMOTION RECOGNITION BASED ON EEG DURING MUSIC LISTENING

Nattapong Thammasan[†], Ken-ichi Fukui, Koichi Moriyama, and Masayuki Numao

Institute of Scientific and Industrial Research, Osaka University,
Osaka, Japan
[†]E-mail: nattapong@ai.sanken.osaka-u.ac.jp
www.osaka-u.ac.jp

We propose a methodology to recognize human emotion by utilizing data from brainwave captured by electroencephalogram (EEG). In this research, music clips were used and 12 electrodes were placed near the frontal lobe of brain according to 10-20 International System. Fractal dimension values were calculated by Higuchi algorithm for constructing feature vectors. Then, features were labeled by time-vary self-annotated emotions by participants in 2-dimensional emotion model. Support vector machine (SVM) and multilayer perceptron (MLP) were applied to recognize arousal and valence separately. From 10-fold cross-validation testing, high/low arousal levels could be recognized with 85.92-89.14% average accuracy. Also we could classify positive/negative valence levels with 90.28-90.83% average accuracy. Additionally, using data from either familiar songs or unfamiliar songs could make classifiers perform 3-7% better than using the data from the combination of both. Therefore, using homogeneous sets of either familiar or unfamiliar songs is recommended for conducting EEG-based emotion recognition model.

Keywords: Electroencephalogram; Emotion; Music.

1. Introduction

Music is a language of emotion. Music can induce human's emotion and emotions can be represented by expression of music. Recently, scientists realize that emotion has strong relevance of the brain and physiological reactions, and the fact makes emotion-brain research become a highly active research area[1]. There are various methodologies to capture information from brain, and electroencephalogram (EEG) is one of the effective tools to capture brainwave on reasonable cost. Based on brainwave data, it is highly possible for machine to identify human affects and emotions in real-time or offline. A goal of music-emotion research is to quantify and explain how music influence our emotional

---

† Work partially supported by "Program for Leading Graduate Schools" of the Ministry of Education, Culture, Sports, Science and Technology, Japan.

states. A system with capability to detect human emotion automatically and effectively could offer good approaches to reach that goal. For instance, in the work of [2], emotion values from automatic emotion detection software using the emotion spectrum analysis method (ESAM)[3] to convert brainwave to emotions were exploited to investigate the relation of high-level music features and human emotions. However, the software was not particularly designed to recognize human emotion during music listening. Besides, the emotions were from experience recall of subjects, rather from elicitation by musical excerpt.

This research proposes a methodology to utilize brainwave information recorded by EEG to recognize human emotion during music listening. In the experiments, stimulating music clips were selected by participants. The musical experiences of listeners in particular song could be different. It involves with kinds of subjectivity issues; e.g. musical preferences and familiarity with the music[4]. Besides, emotion related physiological signals are also different by characteristics of listeners. For instance, professional musicians and amateurs produced different brain signals in spite of elicitation by the same music pieces[5]. Many studies in emotion recognition research based on EEG used pre-emotion-labeled music clips retrieved from standard library, where such emotions were labeled by another persons. The work [6] used sound clips from International Affective Digitized Sounds (IADS) and images from International Affective Picture System (IAPS), and emotional states were classified into positive-arousal, positive-calm, negative-arousal, and negative-calm with accuracy of 92.3%. In work [7], emotion-tagged music were used, and joy, sadness, anger, pleasure emotions could be discriminated 85% accurately. In [8], researchers used both self-emotion reports after listening to sound clips and information of sounds in IADS, and classify positive-high-aroused, positive-low-aroused, negative-high-aroused, and negative-low-aroused emotions. They achieved accuracy of 84.9% for arousal classification and 90% for valence classification. A number of literature studies used emotion labels acquired from another studies or standard library rather than retrieving emotion from participants themselves. However, emotion is subjective. In other words, same music can elicit different emotions in different persons. Therefore, self-emotion annotation is essential in emotion recognition because the technique directly reflects current emotions of listener himself rather than using consensus of emotion to tag emotion label to specific songs. In this research, we focused on the technique of self-emotion annotation by participant in our experiment.

Moreover, human emotional and cognitive states evolve with variable interactions. Emotions are continuously influenced by changing-over-time stimuli[9]. Psychological researchers has proposed schemes describing human emotional states in terms of temporal values[10]. In music listening, especially for the long-length song, emotions could vary since the beginning until the end of the song. Consequently, it is quite crucial to capture continuous changes of emotional expressions and use continuous emotion-annotation rather than global emotion-annotation[11], i.e., one emotion annotation for one music. Most of previous studies allowed only one-time emotion report in one song. It was compromising because the song lengths were short. In this research, however, elicitation with longer music was preferred, thus continuous time-vary self-emotional reports from subjects were introduced to indentify the emotions. We call it "dynamic emotion recognition", which means a system that recognize changing-over-time emotions. This system could be more promising than global-emotion recognition because it is more granular in term of time domain.

The overview of research methodology is shown in Figure 1. To avoid cognitive load due to emotion annotation, we separated EEG signal recording and emotion annotation sessions. Then, fractal dimension value calculation was applied to extract informative features from EEG data due to its success in literature research[8]. Support vector machine and multilayer perceptron were applied to the features to construct classification models. In addition, we investigated effect of familiarity to particular songs based on the hypothesis that familiar songs influence perceived emotions and human annotations in different way that unfamiliar songs do.

Regarding self-annotation, one of the common dimensional models to represent human emotion is arousal-valance emotional model proposed by Russell in 1979[11]. In this bipolar model, valence is represented as horizontal axis referring to positive or negative mode of emotions, and arousal is represented by vertical axis that indicates degree of strength of emotion. Although more dimension had been proposed afterward, the bipolar model is still widely used in emotion recognition research because basic emotions such as joy, surprise, can be located in the dimensional space and it was still effective model in recent works to recognize emotion during music listening[12,13]. We used the two-dimensional emotional model to represent emotions.

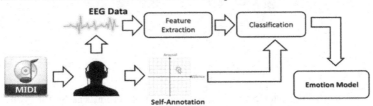

Fig. 1. Overview of research methodology.

2. Data Collection Methods

2.1. *Questionnaire and song selection*

The experiment was conducted with our own developed software developed by Java and the EEG amplifier's software for capturing brain signal. The experiment started with questionnaire about personal information and music related questions. Next, a subject selected 16 music clips as stimuli from the 40-song MIDI library. In the library, eight of song titles were chosen from the most emotional song titles from Moodswings dataset[12], another eight of them were selected from the titles list of songs used in Mr.Emo research[14], and the remaining songs were selected among popular international, Thai and Japanese music library. According to the instruction given to subject, eight of 16 selected songs were the songs that the subject was familiar with, and the remaining songs were the unfamiliar songs. Our designed software offered an option to play short music clip sampled from original music clip in order to facilitate indicating familiarity level to each song, where 1-3 scores denoted low familiarity level (unfamiliar songs) and 4-6 referred to high familiarity level (familiar songs or the song that the subject had known before). Meanwhile, Waveguard™EEG[15] was prepared for recording brain activities. The signals were amplified by Polymate AP1532 amplifier and illustrated by APMonitor brainwave monitoring software[a]. The electrodes were placed according to 10-20 International System. 12 of 21 total EEG electrodes were exploited electrodes and placed nearby frontal lobe of the brain, as shown in Figure 2. The regions of brain nearby selected electrodes are corresponding to human emotion. Sampling frequency was set as 250Hz, and notch filter was turned off.

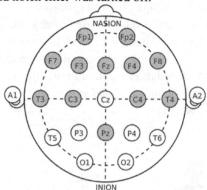

Fig. 2. 12 electrodes placement according to 10-20 International System.

---

[a] Software developed for Polymate AP1532 by TEAC Corporation.

2.2. *Music listening and emotion annotation*

The music clips were played for subject. Each music file had length of two minutes approximately, while this length mainly covered the chorus of song. 16-second pauses were included at the interval between each song for relaxing and avoiding effects from previous song. During music listening with brainwave recording session, a subject spent 30-35 minutes. Then, subject listened to the same songs as previous session again. This time, subject was instructed to annotate his/her emotions perceived in previous session continuously by clicking on a point in two-dimensional emotion space shown on monitor screen (Figure 3). Arousal-Valence emotion model was explained to subject prior to annotate to provide familiarity to the emotion model. Arousal values ranged from -1 to 1, as well as valence values. After finishing emotion annotation of each song, subject was asked to indicate confidence level of previously annotated emotion on the scale of 1 to 3, and indicate whether he/she liked the song or not. Finally, subject was allowed to comment about experiment when all of sessions were completed.

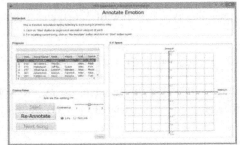

Fig. 3. Screenshot of software for subject to annotate emotion

3. Data Analysis Methodology

The main processes of constructing emotion recognition model was extracting informative features from raw EEG signal and classification based on targeted emotions. A number of algorithms have been proposed so far to identify emotion from EEG signals and to improve performance of feature extraction and classification. Fractal dimension analysis is suitable for analyzing nonlinear systems and can be applied to EEG signal processing as well[16]. In EEG feature extraction procedure in this research, fractal dimension value calculation by Higuchi algorithm[8,17] were applied due to its simplicity. Moreover, the algorithm achieved overall performances in classifying basic emotions represented in two-dimensional emotional space in previous research[8].

3.1. *Fractal dimension values calculation by Higuchi algorithm*

Fractal dimension values (FD values) of EEG reflect the complexity of EEG signal. The Higuchi algorithm calculation generates value that is close to theoretical fractal dimension value from time-series data. For example, given $X(1)$, $X(2)$, ..., $X(N)$ as a finite set of time series, we can construct time series by following definition:

$$X_k^m = X(m), X(m+k),..., X\left(m + \left\lfloor \frac{N-m}{k} \right\rfloor \cdot k\right), \tag{1}$$

($m = 1, 2, ..., k$) where m is the initial time and k is the interval time, then k sets of $L_m(k)$ are calculated as follows:

$$L_m(k) = \frac{1}{k} \cdot \left\{ \left(\left[\sum_{i=1}^{\left\lfloor \frac{N-m}{k} \right\rfloor} \left| X(m+ik) - X(mi(i-1) \cdot k) \right| \right] \right) \frac{N-1}{\left\lfloor \frac{N-m}{k} \right\rfloor \cdot k} \right\}, \tag{2}$$

where $\langle L_m(k) \rangle$ denotes the average value of $L_m(k)$, and a relationship exists as follows:

$$\langle L_m(k) \rangle \propto k^{-D}, \tag{3}$$

Then, the fractal dimension value can be obtained by the slope of logarithms plotting between different k and its associated $\langle L_m(k) \rangle$ multiply by -1.

3.2. *Feature extraction and classification*

We applied Higuchi algorithm to raw EEG signals recorded from Fp1, Fp2, F3, F4, C3, C4, Fz, Pz, F7, F8, T3, T4 electrodes. Sliding windows size was assigned at 1000 (4 seconds), with sliding step of 50 (e.g. 95% overlapping).

We associated each feature of FD values with emotions annotated by subject according to the timestamp. Continuous values of arousal and valence were generated based on the simple assumption that arousal-valence values of emotion of subject do not change until new annotation was performed by clicking on emotional space. We chose only the records from the first annotation of each song until the end of song as input features of recognition model and ignored undecided emotion. In this research, emotions were divided to 2 set of 2 independent classes, which were high and low arousal emotions, and positive and negative valence emotions, corresponding to positions in arousal-valence model. We assigned arousal values and valence to "1" class for zero and positive values, and "0" class of negative values. Until this step, we obtained continuous FD values calculated from EEG data with arousal and valence classes tags. For classification, we constructed two model to recognize arousal class and valence class separately.

4. Experimental Results

In our experiment, the data were collected from 14 healthy male subjects. Ages ranged from 22 to 30 years old. The participants were instructed to close their eyes and minimize body movements while brainwave were recorded. According to annotation results, the average of confidence level of annotation was 2.375, which indicate that we could sufficiently be assured that the perceived emotions in annotated data were corresponding to real emotions. The data were filtered by the 1-30 Hz band-pass filter implemented in APViewer software to extract only desired frequency, e.g. delta, theta, alpha, beta and low-frequency gamma. We applied multilayer perceptron (MLP) and support vector machine (SVM) with universal Pearson VII function based kernel as classifiers for model since the kernel achieved best results in our preliminary research. All classifying algorithms were applied by using WEKA classifier library. 10-fold cross validation was applied for model training and testing.

4.1. *Arousal classification*

For arousal classification, we performed calculation of FD values with every electrodes by Higuchi algorithm as feature vectors as follows:

$$Feature^{Arousal} = \{ FD^{Fp1}, FD^{Fp2}, FD^{F3}, FD^{F4}, FD^{C3}, FD^{C4},$$
$$FD^{Fz}, FD^{Pz}, FD^{F7}, FD^{F8}, FD^{T3}, FD^{T4} \}, \tag{4}$$

where FD^{Fp1} denotes the FD value computed from EEG signal recorded from Fp1 electrode, for instance.

Total number of instances was 107,788, comprising of 65,682 class "1" (high arousal) instances and 42,106 class "0" (low arousal) instances. The results of classification by MLP/SVM are shown in Figure 4. High and low arousal levels were recognized, and the accuracy of 85.95% on average was obtained from MLP and 89.14% averaged accuracy was obtained from SVM. Note that we ignore the results from subject 3 because the subject annotated only "1" class in arousal annotation, and this could bias overall accuracies of classification.

96

4.2. Valence classification

Similar to arousal classification, we also constructed feature vectors by FD values calculated from raw signals of every electrodes. Total number of instances was 107,788, comprising of 76,486 class "1" (positive emotion) instances and 31,302 class "0" (negative emotion) instances. The results of classification by MLP/SVM are illustrated in Figure 5. Positive and negative valence levels were recognized, and the accuracy of 90.28% on average was obtained from MLP and the 90.83% was obtained from SVM. According to the results, MLP gave comparable results to SVM in valence classification.

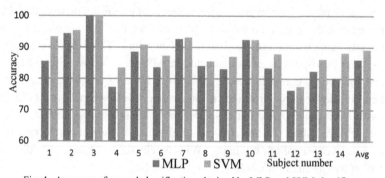

Fig. 4. Accuracy of arousal classification obtained by MLP and SVM classifiers

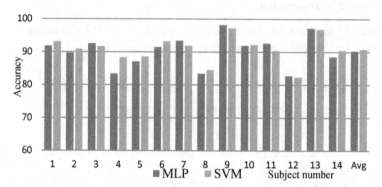

Fig. 5. Accuracy of valence classification obtained by MLP and SVM classifiers

4.3. Effect of familiarity to arousal classification

We divided collected data into two parts, which were data from familiar songs and data from unfamiliar songs. By applying the same algorithm with the same parameter setting, we could achieve averaged performances from each subsystems shown in Figure 6. It is noticeable that by training and testing only by data in subsystem, accuracies of arousal recognition were improved in compare to using the data from the combination of both familiar song and unfamiliar song sessions. Furthermore, the subsystem containing data only from unfamiliar songs sessions outperformed the subsystem trained and tested by familiar songs.

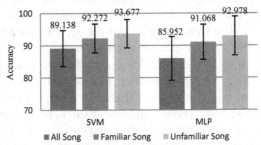

Fig. 6. The average and standard deviations of arousal classification results using EEG data when subject listens to all songs, only familiar songs, and only unfamiliar songs sessions.

4.4. *Effect of familiarity to valence classification*

Similarly, after dividing data into familiar songs related data and unfamiliar songs related data, we applied the same algorithm to calculate FD values from all electrodes to construct feature vectors and we obtained average accuracies of classifications as shown in Figure 7. The results suggested that using technique of separating data obtained merely from familiar songs and only unfamiliar songs were superior to using data from all data in classifying valence classes, where familiar songs could give slightly better results of classification compared to unfamiliar songs.

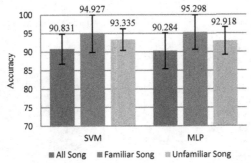

Fig. 7. The average and standard deviations of valence classification results using EEG data when subject listens to all songs, only familiar songs, and only unfamiliar songs sessions.

98

5. Discussion

SVM with universal Pearson VII function based kernel could identify arousal classes better than MLP, and SVM had comparable performance to MLP in classifying valence levels. Our emotion recognition methodology could achieve good results in compare to previous works with the similar methodology[8] (99% overlapping of sliding window; emotion labels were from standard library) regarding to accuracies of classification with the same numbers of arousal and valence of classes. The work [8] obtained the accuracy of 84.9% for arousal classification and 90% for valence classification by using SVM, while our work had the accuracy of 89.14% and 90.83% in classification of arousal and valence respectively by using the same classifier. Despite of high accuracy, however, another methods of testing is to be studied, and the effect of applying sliding window technique in 10-fold cross-validation is still to be discussed.

The best results could be achievable by using only data from familiar songs to valence classifier. After we examined the distribution of emotion annotation by subjects shown in Figure 8, we found quite symmetric distribution of emotions in unfamiliar songs annotation, and we found unbalance to high-aroused/positive emotions in the distribution on emotions in familiar songs annotation. One of possible reason was that background of music and previous experience to music would enhance distinguish ability of subjects between positive or negative emotions, where we could observe that most of annotated data were high-aroused/positive emotions. On the other hand, lacking of background to music for unfamiliar song led subjects to annotate positive/negative emotions quite dispersedly, which could imply to lower levels of confidences of discrimination between positive and negative emotions in ambiguous emotion songs. Moreover, unfamiliar songs could make subjects concentrate to power or strength of the currently listening song, consequently they could annotate arousal levels of current emotion precisely. However, the truth underlying the improvement from separating data and misleading factors are to be investigated in the future work.

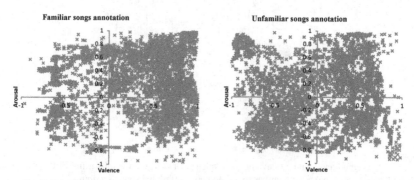

Fig. 8. Distribution of emotions annotation in familiar songs and unfamiliar songs listening

6. Conclusion and Future Works

In this research, we propose a methodology to recognize human emotion during music listening by utilizing information of brainwave. Electroencephalogram was employed and 16 music clips were selected by subject as stimuli, where half of songs in playlist were familiar songs and the other were unfamiliar songs. 12 electrodes were placed according to 10-20 International System. Higuchi algorithm was applied to calculate fractal dimension value from EEG data for feature vector construction. Temporal-altering self-annotated emotions by subjects were used as labels of instances. The collected data from 14 participants were classified by SVM and MLP to indicate arousal and valence classes separately, and we achieved high performance. We could discriminate high/low arousal levels with 85.95% average accuracy from MLP and 89.14% average accuracy from SVM. In addition, we could classify positive/negative valence levels with 90.28% average accuracy from MLP and 90.83% average accuracy from SVM. Furthermore, our results suggested that using either the songs that subject is entirely familiar with or unfamiliar with can enhance the performance of classification, and to use either of them as stimuli is recommended in emotion recognition system constructing.

This research is ongoing work. After acquiring an effective system to recognize continuous human emotions during music listening, the next direction is to analyze high-level music feature and find the relation with changing-over-time human emotion, which was previously studied in the work of [2], while the software used in the work was commercial one and the model parameters were packed together. This approach could provide us better understanding how music influence our emotional states.

References

1. K.A. Lindquist, T.D. Wager, H. Kober, E. Bliss-Moreau, L.F. Barrett, The brain basis of emotion: a meta-analytic review, *Behavioral and Brain Sciences*, Vol. 35, pp. 121-202, 2012.
2. R. Cabredo, R. Legaspi, P.S. Inventado, and M. Numao, An emotion model for Music Using Brain waves, in *Proc. of the 13th International Society for Music Information Retrieval Conference*, pp. 265-270, 2012.
3. T. Musha, Y. Terasaki, H.A. Haque, and G.A. Ivanitsky, Feature extraction from EEGs associated with emotions, *Journal of Artificial Life and Robotics*, Vol. 1, No. 1, pp. 15–19,1997.
4. D. Hargreaves and A. North, *The Social Psychology of Music*, Oxford University Press, Oxford, UK, 1997.

5. C.A. Mikutta, G. Maissen, A. Altorfer,W. Strik, T. Koenig, Professional musicians listen differently to music, *Neuroscience*, 268C: pp. 102-111, 2014.

6. D.O. Bos, EEG-based emotion recognition, *The influence of Visual and Auditory Stimuli*, 2006. Available: http://hmi.ewi.utwente.nl/verslagen/capita-selecta/CS-Oude_Bos-Danny.pdf

7. Y.P. Lin, C.H. Wang, T.P. Jung, T.L. Wu, S.K. Jeng, J.R. Duann, J.H. Chen, EEG-Based Emotion Recognition in Music Listening, *IEEE Transactions on Biomedical Engineering*, Vol. 57, No. 7, pp. 1798-1806, 2010.

8. O. Sourina and Y. Liu, A Fractal-based Algorithm of Emotion Recognition from EEG using Arousal-valence model, in *Proc. of Biosignals 2011*, pp. 209-214, 2011.

9. A. Metallinou and S. Narayanan, Annotation and processing of continuous emotional attributes: Challenges and opportunities, in *Proc. of the 10th IEEE International Conference and Workshops on Automatic Face and Gesture Recognition (FG)*, Vol. 1, No. 8, pp. 22-26, 2013.

10. E. Schubert, Measuring Emotion Continuously: Validity and Reliability of the Two-Dimensional Emotion-Space, *Australian Journal of Psychology*, Vol. 51, No. 3, pp. 154-165, 1999.

11. J.A. Russell. Affective Space is bipolar, *Journal of Personality and Social Psychology*, Vol. 37, pp. 345-356, 1979.

12. Y. Kim, E. Schmidt, and L. Emelle, MoodSwings: A Collaborative Game for Music Mood Label Collection, in *Proc. of the 9th International Conference on Music Information Retrieval*, pp. 231-236, 2008.

13. Y. Yamano, R. Cabredo, P.S. Inventado, R. Legaspi, K. Moriyama, K. Fukui, S. Kurihara, and M. Numao, Estimating Emotions on Music Based on Brainwave Analyses, in *Proc. of the 3rd International Workshop on Empathic Computing (IWEC-2012)*, 2012.

14. Y.H. Yang and H.H. Chen, *Music Emotion Recognition (1st ed.)*, CRC Press, Inc., Boca Raton, FL, USA, 2011.

15. Waveguard: http://www.ant-neuro.com/products/waveguard

16. A. Accardo, M. Affinito, M. Carrozzi, and F. Bouquet, Use of the fractal dimension for the analysis of electroencephalographic time series, *Biological Cybernetics*, Vol. 77, pp. 339-350, 1997.

17. T. Higuchi, Approach to an irregular time series on the basis of the fractal theory, *Physica D: Nonlinear Phenomena*, Vol. 31, No. 2, pp. 277-283, 1988.

PROTOCOL FOR DATA COLLECTION OF MOBILE WIRELESS SENSOR NODES

G. G. Cu

Computer Technology Department, De La Salle University,
Manila, 1002, Philippines
E-mail: greg.cu@delaslle.ph
www.dlsu.edu.ph

S. J. Arriola

Group, Laboratory, Address
Manila, 1002, Philippines
E-mail: shedrick_arriola@dlsu.edu.ph

J. L. Balares

Group, Laboratory, Address
Manila, 1002, Philippines
E-mail: jose_luis_balares@dlsu.edu.ph

K. G. Santuyo

Group, Laboratory, Address
Manila, 1002, Philippines
E-mail: kaydine_santuyo@dlsu.edu.ph

J. A. Yanela

Group, Laboratory, Address
Manila, 1002, Philippines
E-mail: jellie_yanela@dlsu.edu.ph

Aerial Dynamic Assessment Robot for National Advancement (ADARNA) is a research program of the Computer Technology (CT) department of De La Salle University College of Computer Studies that aims to improve the country's disaster response capabilities. ADARNA utilizes radio-controlled helicopters instrumented with high-resolution cameras to see where stranded people and damaged structures are located. The helicopters are equipped with enhanced GPS for image tagging and navigation, and will be fully or partially computer controlled for stability and flight path. Important data is sent to other drones by finding the best path to reach the sink for processing to extract terrain/area features of interest. Since drones have limited data transmission range, the drones have to find a communication path to send the important data to the sink. The objective of this study was to provide a protocol for collecting these important data from the drones into a single sink. The Zewbat data collection protocol lessens the number of total packets sent and the power consumption of the drones. Zewbat piggybacks the data packets by combining multiple packets into a single data packet, which in turn helps with the reduction of the total packets sent. The downside in using Zewbat is there's a possibility of dropping a data packet that contains all the other piggybacked data from different drones.

Keywords: Wireless Sensor Network; Data Collection Protocol; AODV; E-AOMDVjr;

1. Introduction

The ADARNA is a research program of the Computer Technology department of De La Salle University College of Computer Studies which uses radio-controlled helicopters that are equipped with enhanced GPS for image tagging and navigation.

The research program will use a Wireless Sensor Network (WSN) in order to communicate with each other. A WSN comprises a set of nodes that is distributed over a wide geographical area. It enables numerous sensing and monitoring services in areas of vital importance [3]. A remote monitoring application is an example where WSN can be applied. The sensor nodes' locations will need to be tracked, hence, it is the best implementation for a network with a group of drones in an area, since WSN applications are based on the location information of sensor nodes. ADARNA requires a robust and power efficient communication protocol, which ZigBee provides.

ZigBee is a low cost network protocol that is targeted on remote control applications [5]. It is designed to address the unique needs of a low-cost, low-power wireless sensor and control networks. ZigBee is divided into four layers namely, Physical, Media Access Control (MAC), Network and Application layer.

The IEEE 802.15.4 specifies the physical and MAC layer of ZigBee. The implemented MAC layer protocol for the simulation of project ADARNA is Carrier Sense Media Access Collision Avoidance (CSMA-CA). It predicts collisions within a network in order to prevent them [5].

The network layer of ZigBee will use a routing protocol that consumes less power, since ADARNA drones have limited battery life. There are many existing routing protocols that can be applied in the network layer of ZigBee. However, with the need for a lightweight protocol based on the capabilities of each drone, only few of the routing protocols can be considered, one of which is Ad-Hoc On Demand Distance Vector (AODV). AODV is an on-demand routing algorithm that does not rely on active paths and routing information. This protocol discovers and maintains routes only if and when it is necessary. Since it does not rely on any routing information, the different nodes do not participate in any periodic routing table exchanges in the network [4]. AODV utilizes the hop count metric, which means that the path that it chooses is with the least amount of hops. This protocol is not power efficient and it does not consider how much power it consumes when being used.

There are many variations of AODV that exist, which prioritize routing metrics such as energy consumption. The ADARNA system needs a routing algorithm that has low power consumption which the E-AOMDVjr provides [6]. E-AOMDVjr (Energy Ad hoc On-Demand Multi-Path Distance Vector) is an energy efficient version of the AOMDV routing protocol [2]. The AOMDV protocol is an extension of the AODV protocol which acquires multiple non-circulation and link disjoint paths to create a multi-path protocol. The process of AOMDV can be divided into two processes: route discovery and route maintenance. In route discovery, the AOMDV is almost similar to that of the AODV protocol. To ensure non-circulation, an additional variable called radio hops, is used to identify the maximum number of hops. To achieve link-disjoint, the first hop of the RREQ packet is compared with the first hop of the host. If they are different, the routing information will be stored; otherwise, the packet will be discarded. In route maintenance, each node keeps the address of active neighbors, through which packets for the given destination node are received. The neighbor is considered active if it received a hello packet within the last active-timeout period. If a broken link is seen, the source node can restart the route discovery process given a higher sequence number. However, if all links to the destination are broken, it will prompt to restart route discovery. E-AOMDVjr uses an energy balance algorithm which chooses its next hop by identifying which of the neighbor nodes has the least amount of power consumed [2].

The application layer for ZigBee is left for the user to decide, as it will depend on the application that he is creating. The Zewbat protocol utilizes a piggyback mechanism that will be able to send multiple disaster area data in one transmission. In addition, the proponents have also created the Zewbat simulation system which simulates the behavior of a group of mobile sensor nodes in a network that uses the Zewbat protocol. This paper proposes the use of the Zewbat protocol as the application layer for ZigBee.

2. Discussion of Zewbat System

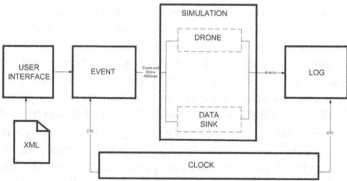

Fig. 1. Architectural Design of the Zewbat System

Zewbat is a simulation system that simulates the behavior of multiple drones deployed in an area and simulates the performance of the Zewbat data collection protocol proposed for ADARNA. The simulator will ask user input that will determine the starting point and flight path of each drone, as well as the different events that can happen during the simulation. The simulation also records several metrics such as the power consumption of each individual drone, and packet and data delivery ratio of the network, which can be used in analyzing the performance of the network after the simulation run. The system also simulates the first three layers of Zigbee and the Zewbat protocol as its fourth layer.

The system is composed of 5 modules: Event Module, Drone Module, Data Sink Module, Clock Module and Log Module. The Event module is responsible for placing the events into the queue. The Drone module is responsible for the initialization of the attributes for each drone. It is also concerned with the movement, sensing and transmission of the drones. The Data Sink module is accountable for collecting the data from the drones and generating grid. The Clock module is responsible for syncing and determining if an event from the queue is to be passed to the simulator at the right time. The Log module takes care of recording all the events throughout the simulation. These modules will be discussed in detail in the following sections.

2.1. Event Module

This module collects the events from Extensible Markup Language (XML) files. XML is designed to store and transport structured documents, which in this case are events and drone attributes. It is responsible for executing the event from the queue once the trigger time of the event matches the current simulation time provided by the Clock Module.

2.1.1. *XML format*

The XML data will be stored in a hashtable, a collection of items that is made up of a key and a value. The value is searched through the use of the key. After getting these data, if the XML contained event entries, it will place the scheduled events in the event queue that are set to occur during the simulation. If the XML file contained attributes of drones or data sink, the program will generate these objects and assign the obtained attributes to those objects.

```
<simulation>
    <event id='0'>
        <type>Drone Failure</type>
        <triggertime>63.35</triggertime>
        <droneid>100001</droneid>
    </event>
    <event id='1'>
        <type>Drone Deployment</type>
        <triggertime>8.46</triggertime>
        <droneid>100006</droneid>
        <macaddress>6fe6</macaddress>
        <speed>1.15</speed>
        <waypoints>
            <waypoint>(95,-190)</waypoint>
            <waypoint>(115,-150)</waypoint>
            <waypoint>(160,-170)</waypoint>
        </waypoints>
        <cameraangle>30</cameraangle>
        <accuracy>75</accuracy>
        <transmissionrange>45</transmissionrange>
    </event>
    <event id='2'>
        <type>Disaster</type>
        <disastertype>0000</disastertype>
        <triggertime>4.0</triggertime>
        <coordinates>(180, -160)</coordinates>
        <width>20</width>
        <length>50</length>
    </event>
</simulation>
```

Fig. 2. Sample XML used for the Events

2.2. *Drone Module*

This module initializes the attributes of the drone. It is also responsible for simulating the drone's qualities. The drone constantly captures data during its flight and is constantly moving based on its flight pattern. The flight pattern for each drone will be based on user input. The transmission of the captured data of the drone is also facilitated by this module.

2.3. *Data Sink Module*

This module is responsible for analyzing all the data that came from the drones. It will determine if the data passed by the drones are significant or not. After the data have been analyzed, the data is plotted into the grid created by this module for the user to view the location of the drone and data sink. Also, verified disaster location is also tracked using the grid.

2.4. Clock Module

This module handles the clock time variable that keeps track of the current and end of simulation time. The clock time is initialized to zero at the beginning of the simulation and is updated throughout the course of the simulation. It checks the different events waiting to be triggered in the event queue.

2.5. Log Module

This module is connected to other modules. It displays the events triggered at a specific time slice. These events include the position of the disaster areas, drone failure, drone deployment, the status of the data transmitted whether it was successfully sent or not, and the data that the data sink receives.

3. Discussion of Data Collection Protocol

The Data Collection Protocol will serve as a representation of the Application Layer of Zigbee. It provides a protocol to support application-level communication. The Application Layer is user-defined and will depend on what type of application it will be used on.

Different Zigbee devices communicate through the use of endpoints. Endpoint acts like a virtual wire that connects an application of one node to an application of another node [1]. The collection protocol uses a piggyback mechanism, which means that when a drone needs to pass all of its stored data into the next drone it will append one data to another. Fragmentation, a process where the data packet is broken down into several pieces, will be applied whenever the data size is too big for one transmission. The collection protocol uses the APSMESET.request primitive, which acts as the form of application level communication between the source node and destination node. The APSME-SET.request primitive will request permission from the destination drone to enable piggyback mechanism. The piggyback mechanism allows multiple disaster data to be appended at a single data packet. The data packet may also be divided into several fragments in case the entire data packet is bigger than the network's bandwidth. The fragments will then be transmitted to the destination node, one by one. Once all of the data has been transferred, the source node will send another APSMESET.request primitive to disable piggyback mechanism.

4. Performance Analysis

Each test case is defined by the following conditions:
- May take form in four different types of topologies
  - All drones have direct connection to sink
  - One path
  - All drones have intersecting coverage
  - Monte Carlo Analysis
- The number of drones per topology may be 2, 5 and 8
- If the test case will use AODV or E-AOMDVjr as its routing protocol
- If the test case will allow the network to use Zewbat or not

Each possible test case is tested 10 times and the results were averaged to provide a non - biased analysis of the system.

Table 1. Zewbat Simulation Parameter Values

Parameters	Values
Area Topology	500 m x 500 m
Simulation Time(s)	200 seconds
Number of Drones	2, 5, 8
Routing Protocol	AODV, E-AOMDVjr
Camera Angle	20 – 40 degrees
Camera Field of View Angle	40 degrees
Accuracy of Acquiring Data	100 %
Range of Data Transmission	10 – 75 meters
Movement Speed	0 – 1.5 m/s
Initial Battery Energy	200 Joules
Transmit Energy	0.0696 Joules
Receive Energy	0.0576 Joules

4.1. *Topologies and Scenarios*

4.1.1. *All Drones Have Direct Connection to Sink*

This scenario has all of the drones present being directly connected to the sink that allows direct routing of data to the data sink and does not require a route through different nodes. The waypoints of the drone are plotted with small distance from one another to allow constant connection between the drones and the data sink. The disaster areas are also positioned to be always within the drone's field of view.

4.1.2. One Complete Path

The drones in the topologies create only one possible path to the data sink. Unlike the previous simulation, which simulates the problem of collision in the channel whenever two or more drones will transmit at the data sink at the same time, only one drone is within the range of the data sink. Therefore, all drones which are not within the range of the data sink must be able to route their data up until the drone which is near the data sink. Another problem may also exist in the topology, when the route breaks due to one of the drones failing; multiple routes cannot exist in this topology.

4.1.3. All Drones Have Intersecting Coverage

The drones in the topologies all have intersecting transmission range.

4.1.4. Monte Carlo Analysis

The following topologies used a randomizer to plot the waypoints for the drones. The first thing done was to divide the Cartesian plane depending on the number of drones needed in the topology. Then first waypoints of the drones are then plotted in their respective allocated area. In order for the drone to head to different directions, angular direction is also randomized, it is computed by using the formula random $* 2 * \pi$. The speed was set to 20 m/s in the randomizer to get a farther distance between waypoints. To get the waypoints, x and y axis points must be computed. To compute for the next x axis point, get the previous x axis point and add it to the product of the speed and Cosine of the current angular direction. To get the next y axis point, get the previous y axis point and add it to the product of the speed and Sine of the current angular direction. Each drone has 10 waypoints in every topology.

4.2. Results and Analysis

4.2.1. Power Consumption

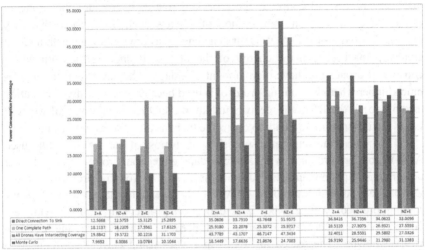

Fig. 3. Power Consumption Simulation Results

The chart shown in figure 3 is divided into three major columns. The first column represents the scenario that has 2 drones present in the network. The second column represents the scenario that has 5 drones present in the network and the last column represents the scenario that has 8 drones present in the network. The four columns present in every major column represents the different cases of each scenario. The first column labeled Z+A represents the scenario that used Zewbat data collection protocol and AODV routing protocol. The second column labeled NZ+A represents the scenario that did not use Zewbat data collection protocol but also used AODV routing protocol. Third column labeled Z+E represents the scenario that used Zewbat data collection protocol and E-AOMDVjr routing protocol. Lastly, the fourth column labeled NZ+E represents the scenario that did not use Zewbat data collection protocol but also used E-AOMDVjr. The different shades of gray represent each topology used namely: direct connection to sink topology, one complete path topology, all drones have intersecting coverage topology, and the monte carlo analysis topology. The chart was arranged like this to easily compare the results of every topology and every scenario. It contains the average power consumption of the drones in the network per scenario.

It is evident in the chart that when using the EAOMDVjr routing protocol, the drones consume more power. The reason for this is that the multi path feature of EAOMDVjr allows backup routes to be created during the route discovery process. Because of these backup routes, it provides the drones a chance to continue their transmission of packets even if the route that they previously used broke. E-AOMDVjr is an energy aware routing algorithm and it creates paths based on the energy of the drones. It chooses the path which consists of drones that have high amount of energy. The power consumption is much higher when this routing protocol is used because it allows the destination to reply to all the RREQ it receives unlike in AODV routing protocol where it limits the destination to reply to one route that has the smallest hop count.

The power consumption results show that most of the scenarios that used AODV routing protocol with Zewbat data collection protocol have higher power consumption than scenarios that used AODV routing protocol without Zewbat data collection protocol. However, for scenarios that used EAOMDVjr routing protocol with Zewbat data collection protocol, it resulted with less power consumption than scenarios that used E-AOMDVjr routing protocol without Zewbat. The reason for this is that when using Zewbat data collection protocol, drones may combine multiple data packets into a single data packet. When this happens, the number of packets sent over the network is lessened and the power consumption of the drones is likely to be reduced. The only time when the battery of the drones reduces is during the transmission and receiving of packets. Thus, with lesser amount of packets generated, there are less amount of packets sent and received by the drones. This is why with E AOMDVjr's multi path feature, the simulation runs resulted with higher consumption of power when using E-AOMDVjr compared to AODV. Using AODV routing algorithm resulted in less power consumption of the drones in the network because of smaller amount of packets generated.

It is evident in the chart shown in figure 3 that using the "all drones have intersecting coverage" topology that has two and eight drones present in the network has the highest power consumption compared to the other topologies. The reason is that when all drones have intersecting coverage, all drones receives the broadcast of packets thus adding to the reduction of power of the drones.

Lastly for the eight drones present in the topology, the topology that has the highest power consumption is the direct connection to sink because of the intersecting coverage of the drones. The topology contributes to the power consumption of the network. The higher number of drones present, the higher the power consumption there is. In addition, if the drones in the topology are set to have overlapping transmission range with each other, the drones are more likely to consume more power because of the packets sent and received over the network. During the route discovery phase of the drones that need a route, these drones broadcast packets to the nearby nodes. The RREQ and RREP received and sent by these drones add to the power consumption of the drones.

The Zewbat data collection protocol affects the power consumption of the drones whenever the data packets got affected with Zewbat's piggyback mechanism. The more data packets it combines, the lesser number of packets are sent and received over the network. The result will then be less power consumption. If Zewbat's piggyback mechanism is rarely used in the network, then there will be higher power consumption because it will not combine a huge amount of data packets and it will not aid in reducing the number of packets sent. The Zewbat data collection protocol does not affect the power consumption of the drones that much. Some scenarios that used Zewbat resulted with lower power consumption while some resulted with higher power consumption. But the results between them are not relatively high. The difference is only a matter of small percentage.

4.2.2. Data Delivery Ratio

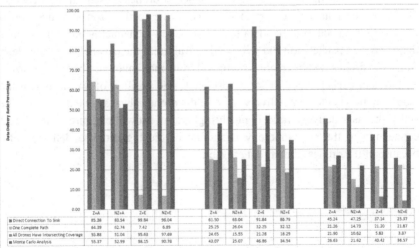

	Z+A	NZ+A	Z+E	NZ+E	Z+A	NZ+A	Z+E	NZ+E	Z+A	NZ+A	Z+E	NZ+E
Direct Connection To Sink	85.38	83.54	99.84	98.04	61.50	63.04	91.84	86.79	45.24	47.25	37.14	25.37
One Complete Path	64.39	62.74	7.42	6.89	25.25	26.04	32.25	32.12	21.26	14.73	21.20	21.87
All Drones Have Intersecting Coverage	55.88	51.04	95.68	97.69	24.65	15.55	21.28	18.29	21.90	10.62	5.83	3.87
Monte Carlo Analysis	55.37	52.99	98.15	90.78	43.07	25.07	46.86	34.54	26.63	21.62	40.42	36.57

Fig. 4. Data Delivery Simulation Results

The data delivery ratio is the number of data successfully received by the sink. It is computed by dividing the data received by the sink to data gathered by drones then multiplied by 100. The data delivery ratio is affected by the number of drones, the flight pattern or topology it uses and the routing algorithm and data collection protocol the network uses. Similar to the previous test, the chart shown in figure 4 is also divided into 3 major columns, which represents the number of drones that were deployed for that simulation. These are further divided into 4 sub columns which identify what type of routing protocol was used, as well as whether or not Zewbat was used. The results showed that using Zewbat data collection protocol and E-AOMDVjr routing algorithm mostly produced a higher data delivery ratio compared to not using Zewbat. This is because E-AOMDVjr provides backup routes for the drones to use to continue its transmission if the routes that it has been using gets broken. Another reason is that Zewbat's piggyback mechanism allows combining multiple data packets into a single data packet. Sending data packet that contains multiple combined data packets have a higher chance to get to the destination than sending multiple separated data packets over the network. The reason is that there is a possibility that in the middle of transmitting all these separated data packets, the route from the drone to the destination gets broken and when that happens, the drone must find a route before it reaches its maximum number of backoffs. Once the drone exceeds its maximum number of backoffs, it will drop the packet it is holding.

As shown in figure 4, the higher number of drones present in the network, the lower the data delivery ratio is. This is due to the drones competing to establish a connection to the data sink first. When a channel is busy, the drones that have data packets to send will need to wait until the channel becomes clear. But if the drones do not create a route within its maximum number of backoffs, all the data packets being held are dropped. The position of the drones in the map also affects the data delivery ratio. If the drones always have a route to the sink, the data delivery ratio is much higher. As shown in figure 4, the direct connection to the sink topology has some of the highest data delivery ratio because of the drones' direct route to sink.

4.2.3. *Piggybacked Data to Total Data Ratio*

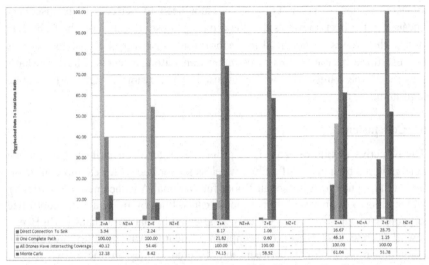

	Z+A	NZ+A	Z+E	NZ+E	Z+A	NZ+A	Z+E	NZ+E	Z+A	NZ+A	Z+E	NZ+E
■ Direct Connection To Sink	3.94	-	2.24	-	8.17	-	1.06	-	16.67	-	28.75	-
■ One Complete Path	100.00	-	100.00	-	21.82	-	0.60	-	46.14	-	1.15	-
■ All Drones Have Intersecting Coverage	40.12	-	54.46	-	100.00	-	100.00	-	100.00	-	100.00	-
■ Monte Carlo	12.18	-	8.42	-	74.15	-	58.52	-	61.04	-	51.78	-

Fig. 5. Piggybacked Data to Total Data Ratio Simulation Results

Piggybacked data to total data ratio is the number of data that used the Zewbat's piggyback mechanism on all the data received by the sink. It is computed by dividing the data received that used Zewbat to the total data received by sink, multiplied by 100. As shown in figure 5, not all scenarios have results because there are some topologies that did not use Zewbat. The Zewbat data collection protocol is used when the drone that contains data does not have a route to the sink to send its data packets to. This mostly happens during the route discovery phase of the drones. Drones that have data in its storage, that haven't established a route because the channel is still busy, must establish a route before its maximum number of backoffs or all the data packets it is holding will be dropped. While the drone is waiting for the channel to be clear, it first stores the disaster data it gathers. Once it has established a route, it will then piggyback all the data in its storage. Zewbat is also used when a drone is holding a packet, due to busy channel, and it receives another data packet from other drones. It then piggybacks the data in the data packet received with all of the data in its storage.

The results showed that the more drones present in the network, the higher number of data are affected by the piggyback mechanism. This is mostly because of the congestion of the channel. The drones, which contain data that are waiting for the channel to be clear, piggybacks the data until a route is established. It can also be noted that using the E-AOMDVjr routing algorithm, there are less piggybacked data because of the backup routes present. In E-AOMDVjr, once a route fails, it does not need to perform route discovery because of the backup routes that the drones can use. Because of these backup routes, the drones do not need to perform route discovery because the drones can use these backup routes to continue transmitting packets. Thus, Zewbat's piggyback mechanism is not often used when using EAOMDVjr routing algorithm.

5. Conclusion

The objective of this research is to provide a protocol for collecting important data gathered by a group of mobile wireless sensor nodes. An example of this is the Aerial Dynamic Assessment Robot for National Advancement (ADARNA), which aims to improve disaster response capabilities by using a radio controlled helicopter to survey an area which was affected by natural calamity. ZigBee, a low data rate and power consumption standard, was used to provide the communication protocol between the different nodes in the network. The Zewbat Simulator was created to simulate the Media Access Control, Application and Network layer in gathering data from different nodes in an area. The simulator allows the user to plot geographical locations of the drones and the sink in a Cartesian plane. The Zewbat Simulator implements a Piggyback mechanism for the Application Layer which will carry more than one instance of disaster data in a single transmission. The proponents conducted several tests which simulated the different scenarios that could happen in the simulation. The general and specific objectives stated were met.

Simulation Results show that E-AOMDVjr produces a higher number of sent and received number of packets compared to AODV. This is due to the backup (multiple) routes that are made. In addition, E-AOMDVjr consumes more energy because of the higher number of packets. The number of data received by the sink is high because there are backup routes that the drones can use even if one of its routes becomes invalid. The piggyback mechanism of Zewbat data collection protocol helps in reducing the number of data packets because it joins the data of one drone with its data during transmission. It also reduces the power consumption of the drones because of less number of packets sent and received by the drones. The accuracy of acquiring data parameter affects the performance in the network in terms of the number of packets dropped. If there is a consistent route from nodes, which carry disaster data, to the data sink, the packet delivery ratio is high because the nodes can easily send the data packet to the data sink, eliminating the issue of dropping a packet due to a broken link. In addition, the number of packets sent is relatively bigger when there are more drones that detects a disaster area. This is because each node transmits their own data packet which may contain the same data sent by the other drones, regardless of the positioning of the drone to the disaster area.

Out of all the scenarios tested, the best combination in terms of highest packet and data delivery ratio is using E-AOMDVjr routing algorithm and Zewbat data collection protocol. If the priority is the data and the power consumption is not an issue, then this combination is best used. The data collection protocol allows one or more data packets to combine into a single data packet. This lessens the total number of packets sent and received by the drones. E-AOMDVjr provides multiple routes that the drones can use to continue transmitting packets to other drones even if the route it first used fails. The downside in using this combination is it has a higher number of packets sent and received that causes more power consumption for the drones. If the power consumption is prioritized and the delivery ratio is not an issue then AODV routing protocol and Zewbat data collection protocol can be used. AODV has a lower number of packets sent but the packet and data delivery ratio is not high.

Zewbat can be further improved by increasing the flexibility of the program by adding different modified versions of the AODV routing algorithm, which focuses on various metrics. Tree-Based Algorithm, a routing algorithm which focuses on dividing the network into several clusters, can also be added in the future to be able to assess which among the different routing protocols is the best suited for the situation. These possible additions to the Zewbat simulator will make the program more robust for different scenarios, as the system will be able to evaluate the performance of the network based on the different routing algorithms that will be added in the system.

References

1. D. Gislason, "ZigBee, ZDO, and ZDP," in Zigbee wireless networking, Burlington, MA: Elsevier Inc., 2008, pp. 207-239.
2. J. Xiao and X. Liu, "The research of E-AOMDVjr routing algorithm in Zigbee network," in *Chinese Control and Decision Conference*, Mianyang, 2011 pp. 2360-2365.
3. M. Matin, "Overview of Wireless Sensor Network," in *Wireless sensor networks – technology and applications*, Rijeka, Croatia: InTech, 2012, pp. 3-24.
4. R. Kachhoria and S. Sharma, "An implementation in AODV based on active route timeout between sensor nodes in wireless sensor networks," in

International Journal on Computer Science annd Engineering, 2011, pp. 1245-1251.
5. S. C. Ergen, "ZigBee/IEEE 802.15.4 summary," 2004, pp. 2-3.
6. N. Gupta and S. Das, "Energy-Aware On-Demand Routing for Mobile Ad Hoc Networks", in *Mobile and Wireless Computing 4th International Workshop*, Calcutta, India, 2002, pp.164-173.

USING MACHINE LEARNING TO PROVIDE RAPID RAINFALL FORECASTS BASED ON RADAR-DERIVED DATA

Panaligan, Daryll* and Razon, Justine Arrnon**

Department of Computer Science
University of the Philippines Diliman
Quezon City 1101 Philippines
*daryll.panaligan@upd.edu.ph
**justine_arnon.razon@upd.edu.ph

Caro, Jaime

Thesis adviser, Software and Service Science laboratory,
Department of Computer Science
University of the Philippines Diliman
Quezon City 1101 Philippines
jdlcaro@up.edu.ph

David, Carlos Primo

Project lead, ClimateX
National Institute of Geological Sciences
University of the Philippines Diliman
Quezon City 1101 Philippines
cpdavid@nigs.upd.edu.ph

1. Abstract

With the recent availability of Doppler radars in the Philippines in recent years, some local groups have taken advantage of the data it provides to generate several new types of weather information, one of which is a new form of rainfall forecast in the country, called rapid rainfall forecasts or nowcasts. Based on ClimateX, one of the first few applications to utilize Doppler radar data, this study used both Doppler radar data and automatic weather station (AWS) data to generate probabilistic nowcasting models by using support vector machines (SVM). Data from 2012, March to 2013, December was used for the training and test dataset, with 80% of the data being used for training. As the only input, Doppler radar data were used to produce rainfall forecasts for each hour for the next four hours from the nowcasting models. The results from several forecast verification methods show that using machine learning to provide rainfall nowcasts is a viable option.

2. Introduction

Rainfall forecasts in the country are greatly lacking in accuracy and reliability. This can be seen in the discrepancy in rainfall forecasts and actual rainfall occurrences. Philippine weather is full of monsoons and typhoons and the unreliability of rainfall forecasts in the country affect the preparedness of the country for disasters which the country's weather often brings. Accurate rainfall forecasting is invaluable in the country since early warnings of heavy rainfall can help prevent the damage caused by severe weather if timely and accurate. The Nationwide Operational Assessment of Hazards or Project NOAH was developed in 2012 to improve the country's disaster preparedness and disaster management against different calamities including typhoons through advanced instruments and methods of science and technology. The Climate Experiment Project or ClimateX helps improve the country's rainfall forecasts under Project NOAH. ClimateX is the first of its kind in the country, providing rapid rainfall forecasts. It provides automated forecasts on almost all of the major locations in the country. It is also the first of its kind in the country in its method of rainfall forecasting. It calculates the (percent chance of rain) PCOR for a particular area by a time series prediction on the movement of rain clouds detected by Doppler radars. ClimateX shows great potential in improving rainfall forecasts, and consequently, disaster preparedness in the country.

This study aims to apply machine learning to current ClimateX precipitation forecasting methods to improve the efficiency of the forecasting method, and to further improve the accuracy of the forecasts. The group was keen on following Project NOAH in its vision for the country. This study would both help the country prevent severe damage caused by disasters and encourage the country to learn to use modern science and technology to improve the country, not just in disaster preparedness and management, but in other areas as well. Rainfall is difficult to predict because of its multi-factorial nature. To construct a predictive system for accurate rainfall forecasting is one of the greatest challenges to researchers. Choosing which machine learning model to use and how to train and optimize the parameters of the model were the most challenging parts of the study. With adequate research, the group was able to decide on using a support vector machine-based model for the study.

This study made use of a support vector machine-based model with an RBF kernel. Basic algorithms for the optimization of the parameters of the SVM kernel and for the training of the model were used. More advanced and more complex algorithms like the simulated annealing algorithm and the particle swarm optimization algorithm mentioned in this study were no longer explored. The results of the project were fairly good with performance slightly better than that of ClimateX. Perhaps more explorations on other algorithms in training and parameter optimization, and further training on new data could improve the performance of the model. The study was successful in presenting a new opportunity for improvement in rainfall forecasting in the country and in supporting the aim of Project NOAH to utilize advanced instruments and methods of science and technology in improving the country's disaster preparedness and disaster management.

3. Review of Related Literature

3.1. *Weather forecasting in the Philippines: PAGASA, Project NOAH, and ClimateX*

The Philippine Atmospheric, Geophysical and Astronomical Services Administration (PAGASA) is the national weather bureau responsible for providing public weather forecasts and advisories in the Philippines. After the country was caught unprepared by super typhoons Ondoy and Basyang (Ketsana and Conson) because of unreliable weather forecasts, the Philippine Department of Science and Technology (DOST) started to develop Project NOAH (Nationwide Operational Assessment of Hazards) to assist PAGASA and to augment the capability of the weather bureau. Project NOAH was developed with the aim to promote and integrate advanced science and technology to enhance disaster management and prevention capacity of the Philippine government which include the deployment of instruments and state-of-the-art methods to construct high resolution hazard maps that are relevant to the community and local government units; delivery of readily accessible, timely and accurate hazards information through various media and communication platforms.[1] New weather equipment including Doppler radars and rain gauges that monitor clouds and amount of rainfall for precipitation forecasting were installed all around the country for Project NOAH. On July 2012, Project NOAH was officially launched, and after only a month, the newly installed equipment and the newly launched Project NOAH both proved to be effective when accurate forecasts and timely warnings were given during an unusual southwest monsoon rains that flooded large areas of Metro Manila and surrounding provinces. The monsoon caused 75 mm of rainfall in an hour which was seen through the use of the newly installed rain gauge.[2]

With the availability of new Doppler radars and rain gauges, Project NOAH provides more accurate rainfall forecasting for the Philippines through the ClimateX project. ClimateX is the first of its kind in the country, presenting a new method in rainfall forecasting. The forecasts mainly come from Doppler Weather Radar data. Different Weather Radars located around the country detect the location of rainclouds, as well as the amount of rain they bring. Forecasted percent chance of rain is done by projecting the positions of each cloud using vector analysis. Besides the Doppler Weather Radar data, historical data, the time of the day, data from nearby rain gauges, and the location of intertropical convergence zones are also considered to predict rainfall patterns. ClimateX provides rainfall forecasts for up to four (4) hours into the future for all major cities and municipalities that are covered by the PAGASA RADAR network. This is particularly useful for thunderstorms which can appear within an hour and last anywhere from 1 to 4 hours. ClimateX has 84% accuracy and 80% success ratio based on an independent accuracy assessment done by COG-NOS team of IBM Philippines.[3] ClimateX is continually being improved to get even more accurate forecasts through comparisons of historical rainfall forecast data and actual rainfall data. Currently, this is done through the manual analysis of data and adjustment of forecast methods by ClimateX workers which can be time consuming and prone to human error. This study presents a more efficient method of improving the accuracy of rainfall forecasts by ClimateX through the use of support vector machines. Machine learning has yet to be applied to weather forecasting methods in the Philippines. No official research related to this has been made known to the public so it is not known whether efforts on applying machine learning to weather forecasting methods in the country have been made. The application of machine learning to ClimateX seems to be the right next step to continue the country's journey towards better disaster preparedness through more accurate weather forecasts in line with the mission of Project NOAH of using science and technology to promote and integrate advanced science and technology to enhance disaster management and prevention capacity in the country.

3.2. *Precipitation forecast and forecast validation methods used in ClimateX*

The Climate Experiment Project (ClimateX) (`http://climatex.ph`) provides rainfall nowcasts for the next four hours by using data derived from

Doppler radars situated around the country. This is done in five steps:

(1) Convert reflectivity data to rain rates using the standard Z-R relations (research more)
(2) Accumulate the obtained data from the past 3 hours
(3) Identify the most persistent vector based on the trail produced by the accumulated clouds
(4) Translate the latest cloud image using the identified vector to produce forecast images for each hour after the current time, for a total of four hours.
(5) Compute the percent chance of rain (PCOR) for target locations by obtaining the percent area covered by the forecast cloud images within a 5km radius from each target location

This whole process takes around 2 minutes to finish. ClimateX updates its forecast at most once every fifteen minutes, depending on the availability of real time radar data. For validation, the data is consolidated per hour. The accuracy, frequency bias, success ratio, and probability of detection of the past forecast data are used for the validation method. The fraction of the forecasts that were correct dictate the accuracy of the forecast. The frequency bias indicates whether the system 'underforecasts' or 'overforecasts'. The success ratio is the fraction of the positive rainfall forecasts that were correctly observed, while the probability of detection is the fraction of the observed rainfall that were correctly forecast.

3.3. *Machine learning and support vector machines for rainfall forecasting*

Rainfall has many factors. Its pattern of occurrence is hard to define since it also differs from a period of time and from certain locations. It has always been a challenge to forecast rainfall accurately. Different approaches have been tried to make accurate future predictions on rainfall and one common modern approach used is Machine Learning where computers are used to create models based on past rainfall data to recognize patterns on rainfall occurrences to make predictions for future rainfall occurrences. Artificial Neural Networks (ANN) and Support Vector Machines (SVM) based models are the popular Machine Learning models used to forecast rainfall using various kinds of input data. In a study held in 2011, Vikram and Veer was able to forecast rainfall in the Andhra Pradesh using support vector regression with swarm optimization algorithm. Vikram and Veer opted to use support vector regression with particle swarm optimization algorithm (SVR-PSO) instead of ANN because they found that ANN had some limitations in learning the patterns because the generalization of single neural network is not unique. In the practical application, ANN often exhibits inconsistent and unpredictable performance on noisy data. Their experimental results indicate that the SVR based on particle swarm optimization and projection pursuit (SVR-PSO-PP) model is superior to the neural network with back propagation (BP-NN) model for the training samples and testing samples of rainfall forecasting in terms of different measurement. [4]

Hong and Pai conducted a similar study on SVR. The study introduces a novel forecasting technique, support vector regression with simulated annealing algorithm (SVRSA), for forecasting amounts of rainfall during typhoon seasons in northern Taiwan. The experimental results reveal that the SVRSA model is a promising alternative in forecasting amounts of rainfall. According to Hong and Pai, reasons for the superior performance of the SVRSA model can be as follows. First, the SVR conducts structural risk minimization rather than minimizing the training errors. Therefore, the SVR model has good generalization ability. Second, simulated annealing algorithms can select the three parameters of the SVRSA model properly to improve the forecasting accuracy. [5] In both studies, the models created provided rainfall forecasts with relatively high accuracy. The importance of the optimization of the parameters of the SVRs in the performance of the model was also emphasized in both studies where special optimization algorithms in finding the best parameter values for the SVR models were given much time and effort. However, in both studies, the features used to train the model were not specified so they were not given much emphasis.

Ingsrisawang, et al conducted a study wherein different machine learning techniques were used with 2 different datasets, GPCM and GPCM+RADAR. GPCM data contained 52 variables or features, for example, temperature, humidity, pressure, wind, atmospheric stability, seeding potential, operation and rain occurrence, while GPCM+RADAR data contained all 52 features of GPCM plus the number of clouds, cloud base height, cloud intensity, and rain coverage area making 57 features in total. It was found that all models perform somewhat better for GPCM dataset than GPCM+RADAR dataset in both predictions of rainfall occurrence and classification of rain levels within same-day period. This indicated that too many or possibly redundant features can cause the rainfall forecasting to be inefficient and lower the accuracy. Therefore, the selection of relevant features and elimination of irrelevant and redundant ones are primarily needed to increase in prediction accuracy and avoid over fitting of the training data.[6] The study shows how the features used in forecasting can also greatly affect the performance of the model.

4. Methodology

Doppler radar data and tipping bucket rain gauge data gathered in a year's time (2012, March to 2013, December) were used as input data and target output data in this study. The Doppler radar data provided the location and amount of precipitation in clouds. The radar is located in Subic (14 49.328'N, 120 21.825'E) at 500 m.a.s.l. with a nominal range of 200km. Radar data for each sweep is produced every 9 minutes for each of the 14 elevation angles. For this study, sweeps at an angle of 1.5 were used - the same elevation angle used by ClimateX in their forecasts. The actual rainfall data gathered from a tipping bucket rain gauge located at the Napindan Automatic Weather Station (AWS) (14 33.481'N, 121 2.641'E) were represented as a binary variable, with 1 denoting the presence of rainfall (mmrain ¿ 0), and 0 otherwise. The rain gauge data is logged at 15-minute intervals with a tipping size of 0.254 mm. If the amount of rain collected during the current interval does not reach 0.254 mm, the tipping bucket rain gauge may only report the presence of rain during the next interval.

The Doppler radar data was read and parsed using wradlib, an open source library for weather data processing written in Python.[7] It was expressed in terms of the percentage of cloud cover in the area within 5km, 10 km, 15 km, and 20 km (%cover_5km, %cover_10km, %cover_15km, %cover_20km). The difference of %cover between adjacent areas (Δ%cover_0km–5km, Δ%cover_5km–10km, Δ%cover_10km–15km, Δ%cover_15km–20km) was also part of the input data. All values were taken relative to the location of the Napindan AWS.

The rain gauge data was consolidated into hourly intervals to match the format of the rainfall forecasts. It was scaled and normalized to optimize the performance of the learning algorithm. Scaling was done to the range of [-1,+1] to avoid large numerical values that may cause problems in computations in the learning algorithm. The RBF kernel of support vector machines used in this study assumes the data to be centered around zero so the data was scaled to the range [-1,+1] instead of the range [0,1]. For the collected data, 80% was used as training data while the remaining 20% was used as test data.

Stochastic, neural networks, support vector machine and logistic regression based models were the forecast models considered for the implementation of this project. Artificial Neural Networks (ANN) and Support Vector Machines (SVM) were the top choices because of their popularity in solving a wide variety of forecasting problems including rainfall forecasting. An SVM based model was decided to be the best option for the particular time series forecasting problem in this study primarily because of its ability to provide unique and globally optimal solutions. The SVM uses the structural risk minimization (SRM) principle to find a decision rule with good generalization capacity which is important in forecasting rainfall where patterns are often hard to find. The training of an SVM is equivalent to solving a linearly constrained quadratic optimization problem, so the solution obtained by applying SVM method is always unique and globally optimal, unlike the other traditional stochastic or neural network methods.[8] In this study, training data consisting of plots of rain clouds acquired from Doppler radars are used to forecast rainfall. It is best that this kind of training data where patterns that produce accurate forecasts are hard to find be approached with a good generalization rule to produce unique and globally optimal solutions.

The principle of parsimony was also considered in choosing the best model for the time series problem of forecasting rainfall this study presents. According to this principle, the model with the smallest possible number of parameters should always be selected so as to provide an adequate representation of the underlying time series data. Out of a number of suitable models, one should consider the simplest one that still maintains an accurate description of inherent properties of the time series. The more complicated the model, the more possibilities will arise for departure from the actual model assumptions. With the increase of model parameters, the risk of overfitting also subsequently increases. An over fitted time series model may describe the training data very well, but it may not be suitable for future forecasting. As potential overfitting affects the ability of a model to forecast well, parsimony is often used as a guiding principle to overcome this issue.[9] A Support Vector Machine (SVM) based model is simpler compared to a neural network based model in terms of its parameters for training. An SVM only has 2 parameters with an RBF kernel while an ANN has at least 4 parameters (the number of hidden neurons, the number of epochs, the learning rate, the momentum etc.) that need to be considered and properly initialized before training.

There are still disadvantages in choosing an SVM-based model over an ANN-based model. One would be the incapability of SVMs to retrain.

Unlike an ANN-based model, an SVM-based model would not be able to retrain and learn by itself using the new data it is input with once it is being used for prediction. SVMs may be less prone to overfitting than ANNs, but SVMs also are not able to retrain and improve itself once it is trained with the training data. The SVM-based model in this study would have to be retrained with new training data and new parameters after some period of time.

The support vector machine-based models created in this study were created with the assistance of scikit-learn, a machine learning library in Python. [10] Four support vector machine-based models were created for this study that forecasts the presence of rainfall for the 1st, 2nd, 3rd, and 4th hour after the Doppler radar data was input which will be referred to in this paper as Rain1hr, Rain2hr, Rain3hr, and Rain4hr respectively. One model was created for each hour. Consequently, there were 4 different data sets for each model. 4 different sets of target output data was used to train and test each model, but only 1 set of input data was used for all 4 support vector machine-based models. An RBF kernel was the kernel chosen for this study to ensure a smooth training of the model. An RBF kernel nonlinearly maps samples into a higher dimensional space so it, unlike the linear kernel, can handle the case when the relation between class labels and attributes is nonlinear. The RBF kernel also has fewer hyperparameters and numerical difficulties than the polynomial kernel — more hyperparameters and numerical difficulties complicate the training. One key point is $0 < K_{ij} \leq 1$ in contrast to polynomial kernels of which kernel values may go to infinity $(\gamma x_i^T x_j + r > 1)$ or zero $(\gamma x_i^T x_j + r < 1)$ while the degree is large. [11]

There are two parameters for an RBF kernel: C and γ. It is not known beforehand which C and γ are best for a given problem; consequently some kind of model selection (parameter search) must be done. The goal is to identify good (C; γ) so that the classifier can accurately predict unknown data (i.e. testing data). In this study, an exhaustive grid search was conducted to find the best C and γ for each of the 4 models using cross-validation to test the accuracy of the C and γ. For each of the 4 training data sets, 10% of the data was used for cross-validation, testing the accuracy of the classifiers C and γ which were trained on the remaining 90% of the data. Thus, each instance of the whole training set is predicted once so the cross-validation accuracy is the percentage of data which are correctly classified. Various pairs of (C; γ) values were tried and the one with the best cross-validation accuracy was picked for each model. Exponentially growing sequences of C and γ, particularly $[2^{-5}, 2^{-3}, ..., 2^{15}]$

and $[2^{-15}, 2^{-13}, ..., 2^3]$ were tried and the C and γ values shown in Table 1 were found to be the ones with the best accuracy. It took approximately 50 hours with a desktop computer* for the exhaustive grid search to find the values.[11]

Using the best values of parameters C and γ of the RBF kernel found through exhaustive grid search and cross-validation, the 4 models were then trained with the Doppler radar data as the input data and the rain gauge data as the target output data. Since the models were trained using the scikit-learn library, a training method called Sequential Minimal Optimization (SMO) was used. The newly trained models were then tested using the test data to determine their performance. A detailed discussion on the performance of the models and the results of the testing are found in the next parts of the paper.

5. Results and Discussion

The generated forecasting models were used to provide both dichotomous and probabilistic forecasts over the location of the Napindan AWS. Using the remaining 20% of the radar data in the dataset, about 14885 pairs of both dichotomous and probabilistic forecasts from the model were produced in order to obtain several verification criteria to measure the performance of the forecasting models. To provide a comparison to a relatively similar forecasting method, the values obtained from the results of the model were compared to the values obtained from a previously mentioned independent assessment of ClimateX. These comparisons were made for both accuracy and success rate values.

To compute the verification criteria based on dichotomous forecasts — namely accuracy, and success rate — the following contingency table was used:

	Observed YES	Observed NO	Total
Forecast YES	Hits	False Alarms	Forecast YES
Forecast NO	Misses	Correct Negatives	Forecast NO
Total	Observed YES	Observed NO	Total

---

*Specifications: 16.0 GB RAM, Intel Core i7 870 quad-core CPU at 2.93 GHz with Hyper-Threading enabled.

Contingency Table - Observed Values					
Hour	Hits	Misses	False Alarms	Correct Negatives	Total
1	630	597	230	13428	14885
2	398	812	215	13460	14885
3	283	922	185	13495	14885
4	238	941	82	13624	14885

One of the simplest verification criteria is the accuracy, given by the following equation:

$$Accuracy = \frac{hits + correct\ negatives}{total}$$

Based on the given values, the model's accuracy was higher than that of ClimateX's in all of the succeeding hours. While this may be the simplest in terms of verification criteria, this can be misleading due to the fact that most of the positive contributions to the criteria comes from the more common category. A sufficient amount of correct negatives, as seen in table 1, easily outweigh the number of hits, hiding the discrepancy between the total number of forecasts made and the number of hits. This scenario is especially true in a rapid forecast scenario where predictions are made every fifteen minutes.

Accuracy		
Hour	ClimateX	SVM Model
1	84.35	94.4440712126
2	82.08	93.1004366812
3	81.25	92.5629828687
4	80.62	93.1273093719

Another verification criteria used to compare the model with ClimateX is the success rate, given by the equation:

$$Success\ Rate = \frac{hits}{hits + false\ alarms}$$

This criteria identifies whether the model is successful in producing forecasts that denote the presence of rain. In the success rates obtained for both forecast methods, it was evident that both graphs showed a downward trend in the values until the 4th hour, where a sudden increase in success rate was observed. As for the performance of the generated forecast models, ClimateX performed better than the model for the first hour, after which the succeeding models gradually started to perform better.

| | Success Rate | |
Hour	ClimateX	SVM Model
1	79.88	73.25
2	64.69	64.92
3	57.49	60.47
4	64.18	74.375

For the assessment of the probabilistic forecasts provided by the generated models, a single verification method was used. Since a single probabilistic forecast cannot be verified with a single observation, one must verify a set of probabilistic forecasts, usually by using the relative frequencies of the occurrence of such events given a forecast probability.[12] A frequently used method for assessing probabilistic forecasts is the reliability diagram. By categorizing each probabilistic forecast into intervals of regular frequencies, an estimate of how well the predicted probabilities of a rain event correspond to their observed frequencies can be obtained. Interpreting the reliability diagram is done by inspecting the location of the points with respect to the diagonal. The reliability is indicated by the proximity of the curve to the diagonal. Points exactly on the diagonal represent a perfect score; points that lie below the diagonal indicate overforecasting, while points that lie above it indicate underforecasting.[13] In the obtained reliability diagrams, it was observed that the system generally underforecasts while following the trend of the diagonal.

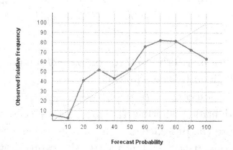

Fig. 1.   Reliability diagram — 1 hour predictions

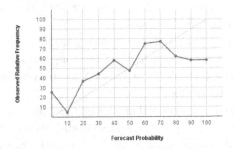

Fig. 2. Reliability diagram — 2 hour predictions

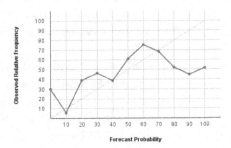

Fig. 3. Reliability diagram — 3 hour predictions

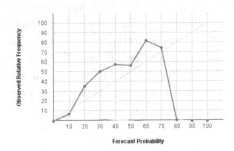

Fig. 4. Reliability diagram — 4 hour predictions

6. Conclusions

In this study, the use of supervised machine learning to generate forecast models from Doppler radar and AWS data to provide rapid-rainfall forecasts, or nowcasts, was described. By generating forecast models from

21-months worth of data through the use of SVMs, the models were able to provide relatively accurate forecasts.

As an alternative to a similar nowcasting method used by ClimateX, comparisons between the performance of the forecast models produced by this study and the methods used by ClimateX has proven the use of machine learning to be a viable option.

However, it should be noted that the method presented in this study requires that a model has to be generated from historical data before any forecasts from newly-acquired data can be made. As previously stated, a large amount of time is needed in order to generate the said model. It should also be noted that the model produced can be used for only a single location. This is in comparison with the method used by ClimateX which requires a smaller dataset, and a smaller amount of time, in order to provide a forecast for any location. The tradeoff between performance and efficiency is evident in the presented method.

Possible future work on the study should explore the effect of using the current date and time when producing forecasts in order to take into account the both the wet/dry seasons and the day/night cycles, respectively. It can also be tested if a greater amount of training data would further enhance the quality of forecasts, since it will include more recurring climate cycles. Also, expanding the scope of the forecasts to several locations could provide a better insight to the performance of the forecasts generated by this method. The idea of using the forecast models in conjunction with the methods used by ClimateX to provide forecasts can also be explored and assessed. Future reviews and insights on this study from experts in machine learning and meteorological sciences could also further improve algorithms used in rainfall forecasting. Especially with the plan of covering the whole Philippines with Doppler radars in the near future, further studies on ways to utilize the information it provides will prove to be beneficial to the country.

References

1. Project NOAH http://noah.dost.gov.ph/.
2. D. Z. Pazzibugan, Weather forecasting in philippines enters 21st century (August 2012), http://newsinfo.inquirer.net/252662/weather-forecasting-in-philippines-enters-21st-century.
3. Climatex: Accurate rainfall forecasting for the philippines (February 2014), http://blog.noah.dost.gov.ph/2014/02/02/

`project-noah-climatex-accurate-rain-forecasting-for-the-`
`philippines/`.

4. P. Vikram and P. R. Veer, Rainfall forecasting using nonlinear svm based on pso, *(IJCSIT) International Journal of Computer Science and Information Technologies* **2**, 2309 (2011).

5. W. C. Hong and P. F. Pai, Potential assessment of the support vector regression technique in rainfall forecasting, *Water Resour Manage* **21**, 495 (2007).

6. L. I. et al., Machine learning techniques for short-term rain forecasting system in the northeastern part of thailand, *World Academy of Science, Engineering and Technology* **2**, 217 (2008).

7. M. H. et al, Wradlib: An open source library for weather radar data processing (November 2012), `https://bitbucket.org/wradlib/` `wradlib/downloads/wradlibdoc.pdf`.

8. L. J. Cao and F. E. H. Tay, Support vector machine with adaptive parameters in financial time series forecasting, *IEEE Transaction on Neural Networks* **14**, 1506 (2003).

9. R. Adhikari and R. K. Agrawal, *An Introductory Study on Time Series Modeling and Forecasting*.

10. S. learn Developers, Scikit-learn: Machine learning for python `http://www.math.unipd.it/~aiolli/corsi/1213/aa/user\_guide` `-0.12-git.pdf`.

11. C. W. H. et al, *A Practical Guide to Support Vector Classification*, tech. rep., National Taiwan University, Department of Computer Science (April 2010).

12. Wwrp/wgne joint working group on forecast verification research (July 2013), `www.wmo.int/pages/prog/arep/wwrp/new/documents/` `Ebert.ppt`.

13. D. Wilks, Statistical methods in the atmospheric sciences: An introduction.

INTERNET OF THINGS: MANAGING WIRELESS SENSOR NETWORK WITH REST API FOR SMART HOMES

F. K. Flores[†], C. K. Magdaong and G. Cu

Computer Technology, De La Salle University,
Manila City, Metro Manila, Philippines
[†]*fritz_kevin_flores@dlsu.edu.ph, christian_kay_magdaong@dlsu.ph,*
greg.cu@delsalle.ph
http://www.dlsu.edu.ph

G. Cu

Empathic Space, Center for Empathic Human-Computer Interaction, 2401 Taft Avenue
Manila City, Metro Manila, Philippines

Ambient Intelligent Spaces are essentially environments which are aware of various phenomena and react automatically based on certain events; as such, construction, deployment, and management of these smart spaces is not an easy task due to its complexity, physical and technological limitations, cost effectiveness, and dynamic environment. The research aims to create a strategy to ease management by using an architecture that includes REST and a node configuration protocol.

Keywords: Ambient Intelligence; Internet of Things; Wireless Sensor Networks.

1. Background of the Study

1.1. *Introduction*

Ambient Intelligent Spaces such as Smart Spaces and Smart Homes, allow intelligence and automation in an environment such as lights automatically tuning on and off, adaptive dimming, and the like. In line with this, innovations in technology allow smart environments to become more realizable due to the development of electronic platforms such as the Arduino Module, wireless transceivers such as XBee, and others. Although ambient intelligent spaces already exists, the current technology is still not ready for commercialization.

[†] Work partially supported by grant 2-4570.5 of the Swiss National Science Foundation.

Ambient Intelligent Spaces use Wireless Sensors, which are comprised of spatially distributed autonomous devices enable applications such as sensing, monitoring, and controlling of an environment. Though powerful, these sensor nodes have limitations in various areas such as management. A few would be that nodes are required to be configured physically for network changes and that node data are typically being sent in plain text and are non-systematic. The research focuses on improving the management for Ambient Intelligent Spaces in terms of on-demand configurability, data collection, and others.

1.2. Objective of the study

The research focuses on creating an architecture using REST as well as another layer used in node communication to enable nodes to be more flexible communication and configuration. The aim of modifying the architecture by means of REST allows heterogeneity in nodes, improved scalability, as well as to abstract the node communication process, leaving a means to simplify deployment and usability for Ambient Intelligent Spaces. Another reason for having the REST architecture is to allow development of applications for Ambient Intelligent Spaces to become much easier in terms of integrating applications to communicate with the nodes in the environment.

Ambient Intelligent Spaces typically use Wireless Sensors Networks or WSN to provide communication between nodes. These WSN protocols such as the ZigBee protocol, focus more on obtaining data from sensor nodes rather than allowing users to send commands to the nodes to allow control and automation. Typical WSN protocols are not specifically built for the use of smart spaces in terms of enabling control and actuation of the environment. The research incorporates the use of three major components; the nodes, middleware, and the data platform in order to provide better management to these environments.

1.2.1. Nodes

The sensor nodes or nodes, are basically modules used in a wireless sensor network. They are made from basic electronics platforms, such as an Arduino Module, coupled with sensors and controllers as well as a transceiver or communication module. An Arduino Module is an electronic platform that allows a customizable and configurable electronics capability for integration with sensors for data gathering and actuators for control. A few of the usual sensors are pressure sensors, temperature sensors, and others depending on the needs of the environment for sensing of certain events or phenomena.

Using a wireless sensor network means that nodes are interconnected through radio waves and data passes through transceivers to allow wireless connectivity. Typically each node is only able to do one task, such as sense or control. The study incorporates the use of these nodes but is modified in a way that it includes a shield or board to be able to accommodate sockets. These sockets allow sensors and actuators to be attached to the node for an easier integration. This allows a single sensor to contain multiple functions in order to decrease the cost and provide an easier way to manage them.

1.2.2. *Sensor network middleware*

The middleware used comprises of the REST architecture and the XBee wireless transceivers. The REST architecture is used in the higher levels of the architecture in the study where the applications and programs are contained. The REST server abstracts the node communication process and allows applications to easily integrate with the sensor nodes. It also provides flexibility in the types of sensor nodes allowing the use of generic components; this is because the REST architecture converts the data into a generalized format. Currently the study focuses on the node communication and uses the REST architecture for an easier and more flexible approach for using the sensors.

The XBee wireless transceiver in the study uses the ZigBee protocol. This ensures a reliable data communication process as well as easier configurability. On top of this, the study also includes a node communication protocol to better manage nodes; functionalities include address clustering of nodes based on location and use, enabling a source and destination communication process, and a generalized node packet data format for sending, retrieving, and control. Clustering allows more than one node to receive data or control sent as well as groups their data according to the configurations of the user. These functions are only a few of the current capabilities of the protocol and may still be improved.

1.2.3. *Data platform server*

The data platform server is used by ambient intelligent spaces to enable processing of data retrieved by the sensor nodes in order to determine necessary action used for automation. With the help of the REST architecture, applications simple use JSON in order to easily connect the applications to the sensor network. The server used for testing is a simple website that contains the node values and controls. The website is only used as a proof of concept in enabling remote control of the environment for monitoring and management.

The nodes used in the study uses Serial COM ports of the server. The website used for testing enables serial port listening to send and retrieve node information from a central node controller connected to the server. The central node controller acts as a communication platform between the server and the sensor nodes to allow listening and sending of information to and from the sensor network. Data sent to the central node are sent to the REST server, which would be relayed to the connected applications using JSON. The study uses the REST server to service the requests of the website and provide replies based on the request in order to mimic actual applications using smart spaces.

2. Architecture and Protocol Design

2.1. *Architectural design*

The architecture used by the study incorporates the use of node controllers allowing unicast, multicast, and broadcast communication to nodes. This is enabled by configuring the nodes to use broadcast mode, but because of the node communication protocol of the study, nodes are able to determine whether data is sent for them or not regardless of being on broadcast mode.

The node controller mediates communication between nodes and the data platform or server. The information obtained by the node controller is then sent to the REST server and the applications would simply request or send data to the REST server to communicate with the sensor network. This architecture allows node information to be concentrated to the REST server, allowing applications to call an HTTP Request through the API to send data to or command to the nodes and back to the server, providing an HTTP Response to the application.

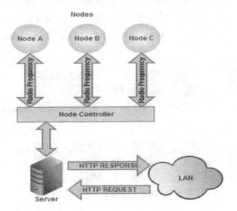

Fig. 1. Node Communication Architecture

136

The XBee transceivers used are configured in transparent mode, allowing plain text serial communication within the wireless network. The ZigBee protocol is also used in the study to ensure reliable communication. Although extremely powerful, the ZigBee protocol requires that nodes be configured physically if there is a change in the environment. Due to this, the study builds an additional layer that is referred to as node communication layer.

The Node Communications Layer, is a custom built protocol layer built on top of the ZigBee protocol for a layered approach. The layer focuses on better management and configuration of nodes.

The REST architecture simplifies data transmission by abstracting the process and converts heterogeneous information into a general and readable format. The API allows applications to easily use as well as enable modularity due to generalization, regardless of sensor, allowing applications to be able to easily integrate management and configuration of nodes in the space.

2.2. Node communication protocol

The Node Communication Layer and REST architecture provides a layered approach, which enable nodes to be comprised of heterogeneous devices thus allowing the use of generic components. This means that over the counter, open source, or locally available technologies may be used as nodes.

2.2.1. Node communication protocol introduction

The Node Communication protocol used is presented as an additional layer focusing in the node communication process. Its purpose is to intermediate communication and enable flexibility, allowing nodes to either listen and process data or simply ignore them if the data is not meant for them.

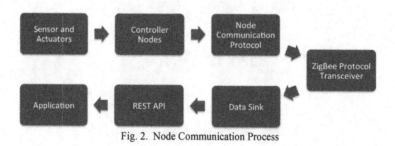

Fig. 2. Node Communication Process

137

The ZigBee protocol, commonly used in wireless sensor networks, although powerful, nodes must be configured physically if there is a change in the network. The study utilizes the broadcast capability of the ZigBee protocol as well as the reliability in communication into the Node Communication protocol. By using broadcast, this allow all nodes to receive all information being sent, but choose to process the packet if it is directed to them or ignore if not.

Using broadcast in the transmission of the data does not incur any significant loss due to wireless being half-duplex. This makes it possible for only one device to send data at a certain moment. Therefore regardless if the nodes were sending point-to-point or using broadcast, the usage of the wireless frequency would be a little or no different.

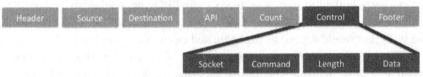
Fig. 3. Node Communication Protocol

2.2.2. *Node communication protocol in depth explanation*

The node communication protocol, which can be seen in Figure 3, is the overview protocol design. It is designated by the study as a node packet, which contains several segments. Each segment represents one byte, however the Control group contains a series of sub-segments dependent on the Count.

- **Header** – denotes the start of the node packet; contains [*FFh*]
- **Source** – value that contains the sending node's address
- **Destination** – value that contains the receiving node's address
- **API** – currently unused but included for development; contains [*00h*]
- **Count** – contains the number of Control groups in a packet from 0 - 255
- **Control** – segment group containing values based on the command
- **Footer** – denotes the end of the node packet; contains [*FEh*]

The API segment is unused but is included for possible growth of the protocol. The Count segment refers to how many times the Control group would appear in the packet. This is used to allow multiple Controls as needed, with the value of *00h* as one group and *FFh* as having 256 groups. The reason for this is to allow a single transmission be scalable enough to contain multiple controls depending on the needs of the environment. The Control group contains the Socket, Command, and Length segments and the Data group.

- **Socket** – designates the socket number of the node in question
- **Command** – contains the code of the task to do with respect to the socket
  - Query Reply – value of the socket replied by the node [00h]
  - Query – queries the destination node of the socket value [01h]
  - Set Socket Reply – value of the socket after being set [02h]
  - Set Socket – sets the value of the socket based on the data [03h]
- **Length** – contains the number of bytes or size of the data
- **Data** – group or byte array containing the actual value to or for the socket

The Socket determines which of the predefined components in the node are being used; including sensors and actuators. For the study, the socket numbers are currently limited to having up to six digital I/O and another six analog I/O with a total of 12 sockets ranging from 0 to 11. This is only for the purposes of the study, but would depend on the board and electronics platform used.

The Length segment denotes the number of bytes contained in the Data group as well as the data type. Lastly the Data group is a cumulative group of segments based on the data contained in the socket. For the study, the values used would be *30h* and *31h* which are the ASCII values of 0 and 1 respectively.

2.3. *REST API*

The nodes are made available through a web service implemented with REST API, using HTTP requests to the REST server. Through this, applications would be able to access node information, control nodes, add new nodes, and send data to the nodes. Application can access the sensors by following the URL format:

http://rest_server_ip/command_type/node_id/param1=value1?param2=value2
- **rest_server_ip** – IP address or domain name of the REST API server.
- **command_type** – command to perform by the REST API server, which is used to access node information, control nodes or register new nodes.
- **node_id** – is used to identify to access the specific node.
- **paramN=valueN** – used as access requirements to process the request.

In accessing the nodes, the following are the command types supplied to the URL in order to perform specific actions with the nodes.

Table 1. Command Type for the REST API

Command	URL	Description
register	http://*rest_server_ip*/**register**	HTTP POST to add a new node by supplying a JSON form data.
info	http://*rest_server_ip*/**info**	Returns node information.
list	http://*rest_server_ip*/**list**	Returns a list of registered nodes.
status	http://*rest_server_ip*/**status**/node_id	Returns a status if the node is accessible or not.
control	http://*rest_server_ip*/**control**/node_id *(add param key if necessary)	Sends a command to the node. A parameter value is supplied that is passed to the node.
query	http://*rest_server_ip*/**query**/node_id	Returns data collected by a node.

Each URL commands returns a JSON response if successfully processed by the REST server as shown in Table 2. JSON is used as a response due to its flexibility as well as is supported by multiple programming languages.

Table 2. REST API Server JSON Response

Command	HTTP Success Response	HTTP Error Response
register	"status": "success", "message":"node_id was successfully added."	"status": "Error", "message": "Error desc"
info	"status:success", "node": [{"id": "node_id>", "description":"node description", "parameter": "parameter values accepted by the node" }]	"status": "Error", "message": "Error desc"
list	"status:success", "node_list": [{ "node": [{"id": "node_id>", "description":"node description", "parameter":"parameter values accepted by the node" }] }]	"status": "Error", "message": "Error desc"
status	"status:available"	"status": "Not available.",
control	"status:success"	"status": "Error", "message": "Error desc
query	"status:success", "message": "node data"	"status": "Error", "message": "Error desc."

3. Performance and Test Results

The assumptions to these tests are; the coordinator is active and there is full connectivity between nodes. Second, nodes use a relay, enabling actuation. The actuation used in the test is to control the lights for sockets 0 to 3; the socket value *30h* or ASCII 0 is off and *31h* or ASCII 1 is on. Lastly, the nodes are configured to use the node communication protocol and set to broadcast mode.

3.1. *Node protocol send and reply test using the query command*

The objective of this test is to determine if the protocol ensures that the data sent is only received by the node or cluster containing the destination address of the node packet. Other nodes or clusters that contain a different address as opposed to the destination address of the node protocol packet should be dropped.

The test is successful. When the node packet was sent from a node, that packet was obtained by the coordinator and then broadcasted to the entire PAN. The node or cluster containing the specified destination address obtained the packet for processing and replied a result, while the others dropped the packet.

Table 3. Send and Reply Test Packet Data

Source Node	*FF 00 01 00 00 00 01 FEh*
	Destination – *01h*
	Control – *00 01h*
	Queries the value of socket 0 from the node *01h*.
Receiving Node	*FF 01 00 00 00 00 00 01 30 FEh*
	Source – *01h*
	Control – *00 00 01 30h*
	Replies with a command *00h* denoting a Query Reply to its socket 0 with a value of *30h* or ASCII number 0.

3.2. *Socket reconfiguration test using the set socket command*

The objective of this test is to determine if the protocol is able to configure the value of a socket contained in a node or cluster. The test also determines if the protocol is able to process multiple Control segments from a single node packet sequentially. The actuation used in the test is turning the lights on and off, where the socket value of *30h* or ASCII value 0 is off and *31h* or ASCII value 1 is on. The result is also a success due to the fact that the desired output is received.

Table 4. Socket Configuration Test Packet Data

Source Node	*FF 00 01 00 01 <u>00 03 01 31</u> <u>01 03 01 30</u> FEh* **Control** – *00 03 01 31h* and *01 03 01 30h* Sets the value of the socket 0 to *31h* and socket 1 to *30h*
Receiving Node	*FF 01 00 00 01 <u>00 02 01 31</u> <u>01 02 01 30</u> FEh* **Control** – *00 02 01 31h* and *01 02 01 30h* Replies with a command of *02h* denoting a Set Socket Reply to socket 0 now with a value of *31h* and socket 1 now with a value of *30h*

3.3. Combination packet sending test

The objective of this test is to determine if the protocol is able to take into account multiple Control segments with varying commands from within a single node packet and process them sequentially. The result of the test is successful since regardless of combining the commands the desired output is still received.

Table 5. Combination Test Packet Data

Source Node	*FF 00 01 00 02 <u>00 03 01 30</u> <u>00 03 01 31</u> <u>00 01</u> FEh* Set the value of socket 0 to *30h* then set it to *31h*, afterwards, query the value of socket 0
Receiving Node	*FF 01 00 00 02 <u>00 02 01 30</u> <u>00 02 01 31</u> <u>00 00 01 31</u> FEh* Replies with socket 0 updating to a value of *30h* and then updated again with the value of *31h*, then a Query Reply value of the *31h* which is the current value of socket 0

4. Conclusion and Future Work

The Ambient Intelligent Space, having numerous capabilities also has a handful problems, one of which in the field of management. The study has been successful in providing better management capability to these environments using the REST architecture and the Node Communication Protocol.

The Node Communication Protocol used by the study is still at its early stages. Although its current capability already allows easier communication and management simply by allowing nodes to determine whether data is sent for them or not regardless of the ZigBee protocol limitations in requiring the nodes to be physically preconfigured. The protocol also allows setting of the data on the node sockets as well as to query them of their current value. Although results have been promising, the flaw of the protocol is that, configuration only exists while the node has power and has its configuration intact, once the node resets, the configuration default back to the initial configured state.

Future works may include improvement of the protocol by providing data prioritization, communication speedup, and others. Other works may include using the basic 802.15.4 protocol for communication rather than using the ZigBee protocol, due to the fact that the ZigBee protocol is not specifically build for ambient intelligent spaces and may incur a slower communication rate. Although results have been promising, the study is still at its early stages and there are still plenty of works to be accomplished in an endeavor to completely enhance the management and configuration process of smart environments.

References

1. Akyildiz I., Su W., Sankarasubramaniam Y., and Cayirci E. (2001) "Wireless Sensor Networks: A Survey"
2. Mahmod A., Shie K., Khatoon S., and Xiao M. (February 2013) "Data Mining Techniques for Wireless Sensor Networks: A Survey".
3. Molla M. and Ahamed S. (2006) "A Survey of Middleware for Sensor Network and Challenges"
4. Romer K. and Mattern F. (December 2004) "The Design Space for Wireless Sensor Networks"
5. Suh C., Ko Y., Lee C., and Kim H. (No Date) "The Design and Implementation of Smart Sensor-based Home Networks"
6. Surie D., Laguionie O., and Pederson T. (2008) "Wireless Sensor Networking of Everyday Objects in a Smart Home Environment"
7. Xu M., Ma L., Xia F., Yuan T., Qian J., and Shao M. (No Date) "Design and Implementation of a Wireless Sensor Network for Smart Homes"
8. Ganesan D., Cerpa A., Ye W., Yu Y., Zhao J. and Estrin D. (December 2003) "Networking issues in wireless sensor networks"
9. Lanthaler M. (No Date) "Self-Healing Wireless Sensor Networks"
10. Law Y. and Havinga P (2005) "How to Secure a Wireless Sensor Network"
11. Karl H. and Willig A. (2005) "Protocols and Architectures for Wireless Sensor Networks"
12. Rulokowski P., Martinez R., and Barrett J. (December 2003) "Sensor Network Hardware Infrastructure for Smart Spaces"
13. Ucklemann D., Harrison M., and Michahelles F. (2011) "Architecting the Internet of Things"
14. Zhou H. (2013) "The Internet of Things in the Cloud: A Middleware Perspective"

AUTHOR INDEX